Dungeon Master II™

The Legend of Skullkeep

The Official Adventurer's Guide

NOW AVAILABLE FROM PRIMA

Computer Game Books

The 7th Guest: The Official Strategy Guide

Aces Over Europe: The Official Strategy Guide

Aegis: Guardian of the Fleet—The Official Strategy Guide

Armored Fist: The Official Strategy Guide

Betrayal at Krondor: The Official Strategy Guide

CD-ROM Games Secrets, Volume 1

Computer Adventure Games Secrets

DOOM Battlebook

DOOM II: The Official Strategy Guide

Dracula Unleashed: The Official Strategy Guide & Novel

Front Page Sports Baseball '94: The Official Playbook

Front Page Sports Football Pro '95: The Official Playbook

Harpoon II: The Official Strategy Guide

King's Quest VII: The Unauthorized Strategy Guide

Lemmings: The Official Companion (with disk)

Master of Orion: The Official Strategy Guide

Microsoft Flight Simulator: The Official Strategy Guide

Microsoft Golf: The Official Strategy Guide

Microsoft Space Simulator: The Official Strategy Guide

Might and Magic Compendium: The Authorized Strategy Guide for Games I, II, III, and IV

Myst: The Official Strategy Guide

Outpost: The Official Strategy Guide

Pagan: Ultima VIII—The Ultimate Strategy Guide

Panzer General: The Official Strategy Guide

Prince of Persia: The Official Strategy Guide

Quest for Glory: The Authorized Strategy Guide

Rebel Assault: The Official Insider's Guide

Return to Zork Adventurer's Guide

Shadow of the Comet: The Official Strategy Guide

Sherlock Holmes, Consulting Detective: The Unauthorized Strategy Guide

Sid Meier's Civilization, or Rome on 640K a Day

Sid Meier's Colonization: The Official Strategy Guide

SimCity 2000: Power, Politics, and Planning

SimEarth: The Official Strategy Guide

SimFarm Almanac: The Official Guide to SimFarm

SimLife: The Official Strategy Guide

SSN-21 Seawolf: The Official Strategy Guide

Strike Commander: The Official Strategy Guide and Flight School

Stunt Island: The Official Strategy Guide

SubWar 2050: The Official Strategy Guide

The Legend of Skullkeep The Official Strategy Guide

TIE Fighter: The Official Strategy Guide

Ultima: The Avatar Adventures

Ultima VII and Underworld: More Avatar Adventures

Under a Killing Moon: The Official Strategy Guide

Wing Commander I and II: The Ultimate Strategy Guide

X-COM UFO Defense: The Official Strategy Guide

X-Wing Collector's CD-ROM: The Official Strategy Guide

How to Order:

For information on quantity discounts contact the publisher: Prima Publishing, P.O. Box 1260BK, Rocklin, CA 95677-1260; (916) 632-4400. On your letterhead include information concerning the intended use of the books and the number of books you wish to purchase. For individual orders, turn to the back of the book for more information.

The Legend of Skullkeep

The Official Adventurer's Guide

John P. Withers

PRIMA PUBLISHING

ISBN: 1-55958-712-1

Library of Congress Catalog Card Number: 94-68407

Printed in the United States of America

95 96 97 98 BB 10 9 8 7 6 5 4 3

Table of Contents

Acknowledgments

There are many players in making a book, and an author is only a small part of a very large team that makes the book happen. In the case of this book, the author has had the exceptional luck of having a team of absolute stone-cold pros assisting him every step of the way. I would like to give credit to some of the most valuable players on the team.

First, Ed Dille, who hooked me up with the people, the know-how, and the superior attitude needed to get by in the strange world of computer game-book writing.

Without the excellent play testing assistance of Tony Morman there wouldn't have been a book.

The incredibly talented Becky Freeman was the project editor for this tome, and her assistance went way beyond the call of duty for a normal human being.

Bill Kunkel and Lori Yates were always there for advice and assistance at some really unreasonable hours.

Rusty Bouchert and Bill Church of Interplay provided excellent company support.

Arnie Katz and Joyce Worley have given me a tremendous amount of support in my career. Without their assistance, it is extremely unlikely that I would have been in the right place at the right time to make this book happen.

Andy Swann should get some sort of special campaign medal not only for his administrative skill, but also for his ability to deal with me in the office before I have had coffee in the morning. That sort of thing has driven lesser men postal.

And, lastly (in case you're still reading at this point), I would like to thank all the friends of Bill, wherever you may be, but particularly in Huntington, West Virginia. You know what for.

Foreword

When we decided to make Dungeon Master II, we faced quite a challenge. Dungeon Master was a ground-breaking game with a huge following. Our challenge was to create a game that belonged in the same line, lived up to all the best qualities of Dungeon Master and somehow was even better.

The first and most important step in this process was to maximize on our strongest resource, our players. Instead of trying to design Dungeon Master II in a vacuum, we let the players guide us. We contacted them, talked to them, lurked on message boards and saw what our players liked the best, and the least, about Dungeon Master.

Another thing feedback told us to concentrate on was to create the best puzzle-solving adventure possible. Instead of a scripted path, we created a world. And in this world more than one path to the final goal exists. There isn't a set pattern the adventurer must take. Instead, you solve the puzzles in the most creative manner you can. You choose your own path to the goal.

We tried to make the interface even more intuitive. No one wants to be rudely jerked back to reality because the command structure is so clunky that you have to concentrate more on your cursor than on playing the game. Nothing should detract from the game experience.

Finally, we took our time. In today's world, there is a great pressure to rush a game to market. Dungeon Master fans deserved every ounce of time and creative energy we had. And that is what we gave them. We took all the time we needed to produce a product that was well thought out, creatively rich and exhaustively play tested. We hope that you find as much joy in playing Dungeon Master II as we did in making it.

Interplay Productions

Introduction

Forsooth! The young hero. Tornam, by name, are you not! Barkeep, another round for my young friend. My name is Alran the semi-wise, son of Alran the fairly clumsy and not to be confused with my brother, Alren the extremely dim. There, now. With all that out of the way — would you mind paying the barkeep, my changepurse seems to be tangled in my robe — I guess you are asking yourself, who is this old man, and what is he doing at my table when I am resting and girding for my coming battle!

Well, my friend, let me tell you, lucky it is that we should meet on this dark and evil night. My world was attacked by Dragoth in much the same manner as yours. Yes, the evil one activated a dimensional portal and came through with his hordes, overrunning our prosperous land.

And a sad thing it was. At first we thought it might be business as usual, you know: new demonic despot, same old night life. But nay. He performed all manner of despicable acts — killing off most of the serfs, ruining the environment. When the pubs were restricted to minor demons only, I knew it was time to go.

Hence I began to look for a way to a new land where the pubs were — er, to, uh, go out and warn the next dimension along the portal pathway about the evil danger. Yes, that's it, to warn you.

So I went to the great library at Swann, where I poured though the stacks day and night, until finally I happened to find a dusty, ancient tome deep in the darkest subvault of the great underground storage catacombs. And my hand shook as I hefted the great book to the light, for, with my mystical aura, I knew even before I examined it that this was the right manuscript.

Examining it in the flickering glow of my lamp, I confirmed that this indeed was the book I sought. For on the spine it said, "Traveling The Dimensions For Fun And Profit: A Second-Rate Sorcerer's Guide."

Upon finding this grimore, I wasted no time. Rapidly my mind memorized the spell of traveling therein. I grabbed my notes from our earlier unsuccessful attempt to stop Dragoth, my drawings of the maps of the realm, and various magickly inscribed pictures. Then I carved the mystic runes of the transportation spell: HEIS, IN, and BERG. In a flash of light and smoke, I found myself here.

Wait! Don't dismiss me as a crank yet, for I know many things you will need to be aware of on your perilous mission. You heroes are all the same, wanting to run out and lop something's head off without due preparation.

Your world and mine are the same. Same forbidding castle in the center of everything, same sleeping vaults, same magick for spells, same slightly thick heroes. And I was there when Dragoth first started activating my world's Zo Link. I was one of the first awakened to help defeat him.

Betcha you wouldn't have thought that now, would you! But you didn't know me in my younger days. Ah, yes, quite the impressive sorcerer I was in my time, firm jaw, great flowing robes with those stars and moons that the guild makes us wear, piercing eyes. Yes, the hero who led our quest, Tanic, came to my sleeping chamber and said right off, there's the sorcerer for me.

Well, I am sure he felt that way. Impressed, that is.

Anyway, the point is that I was in his party. And we went the distance. I know every nook and cranny of the castle and surrounding lands and how to get to them. I mean we had that slight problem there at the end. Didn't quite kill Dragoth when push came to shove, but we got an "A" for effort. Did quite well I think, all things considered. Except for that last bit where, in a heroic and grand fashion... well, we failed.

But if you just give me a minute of your time here — Barkeep, another round for my young friend, he looks positively parched — I think I can tell you everything you will need to know.

First I will tell you of classes and parties and fighting and all the things you need to know to get out of the sleeping chambers. And I can also impart the wisdom of spells and the various items you will find around the kingdom. And there are the maps I drew of the entire realm. Finally, I will tell you the tale of our adventures and how we found the way out of each area of the realm until finally we came face to face with Dragoth himself and in a blaze of heroic glory, well, we got mauled.

But it will be a long and arduous telling, and I am sure we will get thirsty along the way. Barkeep!

THROUGHOUT THE VOLUME, NOTES THAT APPEAR LIKE THIS TEXT ARE DIRECT INSTRUCTIONS TO THE PLAYER. THIS IS RESERVED FOR KEYBOARD COMMAND DATA OR STATISTICS ABOUT INFORMATION THAT MAY BE NEEDED BY THE PLAYER DIRECTLY, AS OPPOSED TO INFORMATION THAT MAY BE ASSIMILATED BY THEIR ALTER EGO, TORHAM.

I ALSO REALIZE THAT THERE ARE THOSE HEROES WITHOUT THE CONCENTRATION REQUIRED TO FOLLOW MY WORDS OF WISDOM. I AM SURE IT HAS NOTHING TO DO WITH MY BEING LONG-WINDED. HOWEVER, UNDERSTANDING THIS, I WILL EMPHASIZE CERTAIN CRITICAL INSTRUCTIONS WITH HINT BLOCKS TO MAKE SURE THE POINT DOESN'T GET OVERLOOKED IN MY BRILLIANT AND PERCEPTIVE TALE.

The Adventurers

Ah, yes, the sleeping chamber. This is where the awesome adventure began. I remember when Tanic first awoke me and told me of our great mission. How the fire boiled in my blood. Well, maybe I was a bit hesitant there at first. Who wouldn't be! Fighting an interdimensional demon isn't exactly something one just jumps right into now, is it!

As a matter of fact I rather distinctly remember I was trying to duck out the side door to find a friendly pub when Tanic grabbed me by the cowl and dragged me back in. I explained to him that I was merely going to fortify myself for our coming battle and to think out a plan of attack. He scowled and alluded to how he needed my help in selecting our fellow adventurers. Then he bolted the door.

Yes, and that was when the fire rose up in my blood. Yes it did. Ready to kill for the cause.

But there is really quite a bit involved in understanding how to build a party, and we didn't take the time to do it right. Personally, I think that was a major part of our grand and heroic, er, moshing: bad personnel selection.

But the tale of our woe is a long one, and you will have time to hear it at length before the night is out. First of all, we need to deal with the matter of classes.

Classes

Each adventurer starts with a certain amount of skill in at least one of the four classes.

Fighter

Fighters are your basic hack-and-slash infantry of the realm. While at the start of things fighting is a pretty fundamental activity, as fighters progress, they acquire more attack forms. For example, an ax has swing and chop as basic attack functions. But, around Craftsman level, a fighter gets a third option: melee.

Melee is the nasty business of stepping in and doing all those brutish, fighting tricks to the opponent. And, as a result, it can do heinous damage. Melee is slower than swing and chop, but does such a great deal of damage that it is well worth the extra time.

Ninja

Ninjas are stealthy fighters. They are the masters who fire missiles and throw things at people. Ninjas are also able to fight with open-hand attacks. While at first open-hand attacks don't do too much, at later stages of development an open-hand fighter can be a formidable opponent. One major advantage of this attack form is speed. The open-hand fighter hits more quickly than any weapon.

Priest

Priests are spell-casters who specialize in the wimpy type spells. You know, healing, shield, and the like. However, the more powerful priest spells have a minimum skill requirement and cannot be cast successfully at lower levels even with a great deal of mana. The key to solving this problem is to get plenty of practice with weaker spells before moving to the more powerful incantations.

Wizard

Wizards are the finest and highest class to ever walk the planet. As a matter of a fact, there is a distinct possibility that our class was created by the higher power of the universe just so it could show up the rest of the classes. (But there are those who say I might be biased.) Wizards operate under the same general rules and skill restraints as Priests. However, our spells such as combat and door-opening tend to be more directly useful to a party. Wizards and Priests both must be protected early in their development to ensure they can grow into their full potential. But more about that later.

Level Titles

There is a range of titles that reflect the level of ability in the particular class. They progress as follows:

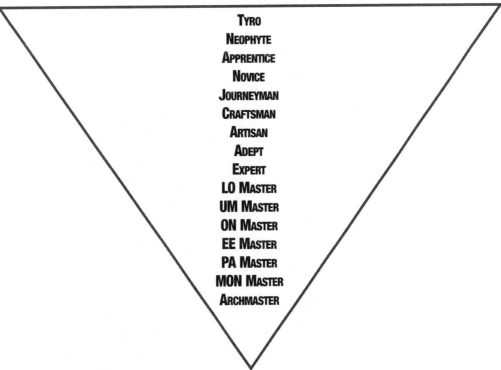

TYRO
NEOPHYTE
APPRENTICE
NOVICE
JOURNEYMAN
CRAFTSMAN
ARTISAN
ADEPT
EXPERT
LO MASTER
UM MASTER
ON MASTER
EE MASTER
PA MASTER
MON MASTER
ARCHMASTER

As the character progresses in a class, the abilities associated with that class increase. Fighters receive more fighting options, Ninjas gain speed, and Magick users become more adept at casting powerful spells.

Seeing an adventurer's statistics while the adventurer is in the stasis chamber can give you a rough idea of how quickly those numbers will rise. Heroes with low numbers in some statistics will tend to stay lower in those areas throughout the game, as compared to those with higher statistics, which reflect more natural talent in a given area. Those with high numbers will rise in a skill more quickly and easily.

But do not forget that skills are flexible. The more a particular ability is used, the more it will increase, even if an adventurer starts with a low score. Thus, everyone in a party will have the chance to improve their abilities at least somewhat in each area.

The minor tome of wisdom from the wizard Interplay already explains the various statistics and what they effect in detail. However, it might be good to restate that speed and dexterity are the important statistics for Fighters and Ninjas. Wisdom and Mana are the most critical statistics for Priests and Wizards.

Party Selection

Now, with a good understanding of the classes and skills, it is time to look more closely at the individual heroes and select the ones that will work best in your grand battle.

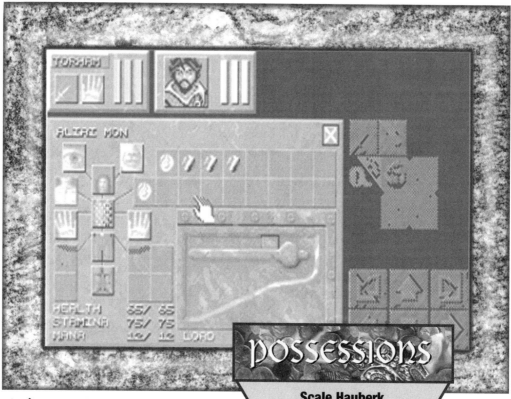

Aliai Mon

Aliai is about as average as you can get. He has no serious weaknesses or strengths. Capable of specializing or becoming an all-purpose utility member, he can fit in well anywhere with some practice.

POSSESSIONS

Scale Hauberk
Leather Pants
Leather Boots
3 Silver Coins
2 Gold Coins

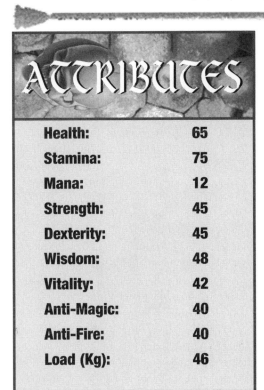

ATTRIBUTES

Health:	65
Stamina:	75
Mana:	12
Strength:	45
Dexterity:	45
Wisdom:	48
Vitality:	42
Anti-Magic:	40
Anti-Fire:	40
Load (Kg):	46

STATS

Class: Fighter
Level: Neophyte

Swing:	2
Thrust:	1
Club:	1
Parry:	1

Class: Priest
Level: Neophyte

Identify:	2
Heal:	1
Influence:	1
Defend:	1

Class: Ninja
Level: Neophyte

Fight:	1
Throw:	1
Shoot:	1

Class: Wizard
Level: Neophyte

Fire:	2
Air:	1
Earth:	1
Water:	1

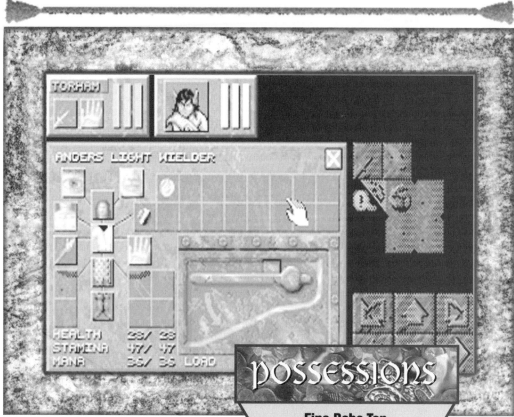

Anders, Light Wielder

Anders is particularly missile prone. A skulk-in-the-back and fling-things-at-the-enemy kind of guy. I rather like that in a hero. However, if he is put up front before he has fully developed his skills, Anders is most likely to end up being field rations.

POSSESSIONS

Fine Robe Top
Scale Mail
Black Boots
Torch
1 Silver Coin
1 Gold Coin

ATTRIBUTES

Health:	28
Stamina:	47
Mana:	36
Strength:	33
Dexterity:	59
Wisdom:	45
Vitality:	55
Anti-Magic:	55
Anti-Fire:	30
Load (Kg):	

STATS

Class: Fighter
Level: Tyro

Swing:	0
Thrust:	0
Club:	0
Parry:	2

Class: Priest
Level: Tyro

Identify:	2
Heal:	0
Influence:	0
Defend:	0

Class: Ninja
Level: Novice

Fight:	0
Throw:	0
Shoot:	0

Class: Wizard
Level: Apprentice

Fire:	3
Air:	5
Earth:	3
Water:	2

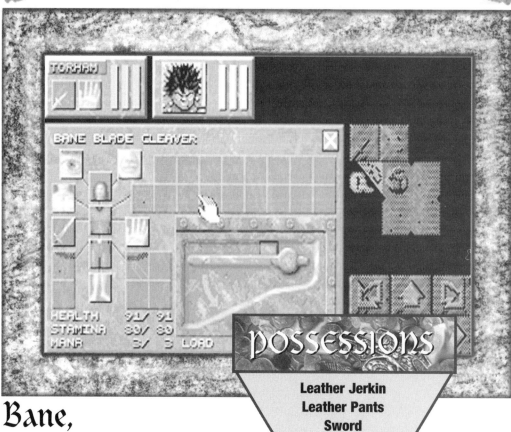

Bane,
Blade Cleaver

As his name suggests, Bane is a destroyer. If he specializes in fighting with his hands, this man becomes a veritable one-man slaughterhouse. Spell-casting is a far reach for him, however.

possessions

Leather Jerkin
Leather Pants
Sword

ATTRIBUTES

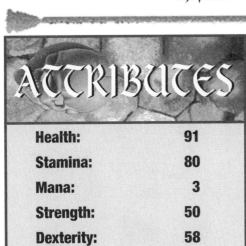

Health:	91
Stamina:	80
Mana:	3
Strength:	50
Dexterity:	58
Wisdom:	39
Vitality:	49
Anti-Magic:	30
Anti-Fire:	30
Load (Kg):	50

STATS

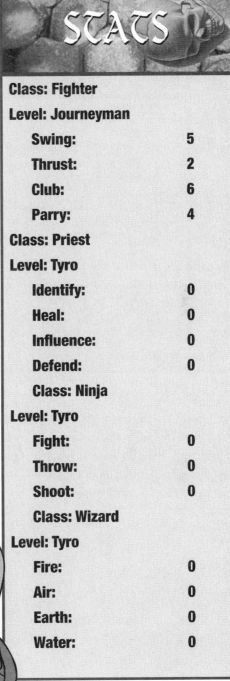

Class: Fighter
Level: Journeyman

Swing:	5
Thrust:	2
Club:	6
Parry:	4

Class: Priest
Level: Tyro

Identify:	0
Heal:	0
Influence:	0
Defend:	0

Class: Ninja
Level: Tyro

Fight:	0
Throw:	0
Shoot:	0

Class: Wizard
Level: Tyro

Fire:	0
Air:	0
Earth:	0
Water:	0

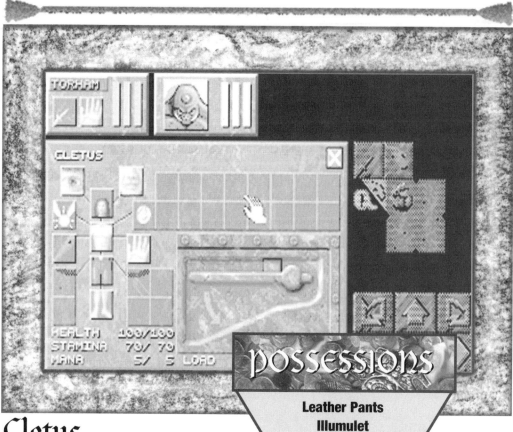

Cletus

It is most fortunate that Cletus is on your side. Bulging with muscle, this was the man voted "most likely to eat through a door" in his class at the fighter academy. But like most of his kind, Cletus won't find the search for mana a pleasant journey.

POSSESSIONS

Leather Pants
Illumulet
Club
1 Gold Coin

ATTRIBUTES

Health:	100
Stamina:	70
Mana:	5
Strength:	60
Dexterity:	30
Wisdom:	32
Vitality:	50
Anti-Magic:	40
Anti-Fire:	63
Load (Kg):	58

STATS

Class: Fighter
Level: Apprentice

Swing:	3
Thrust:	0
Club:	5
Parry:	0

Class: Priest
Level: Tyro

Identify:	0
Heal:	0
Influence:	0
Defend:	0

Class: Ninja
Level: Novice

Fight:	4
Throw:	2
Shoot:	0

Class: Wizard
Level: Tyro

Fire:	0
Air:	0
Earth:	2
Water:	0

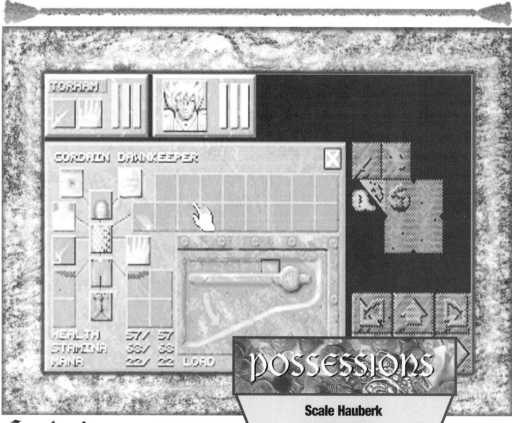

Cordain, Dawnkeeper

Cordain is another all-purpose adventurer with above-average magickal potential. Better armed and armored than most of the sleepers, this Magickal Fighter also has a strong resistance to attacks of many kinds.

POSSESSIONS

Scale Hauberk
Leather Pants
Black Boots
Rapier
Money Box
Containing
1 Silver Coin
and
2 Gold Coins

ATTRIBUTES

Health:	57
Stamina:	68
Mana:	22
Strength:	35
Dexterity:	40
Wisdom:	42
Vitality:	40
Anti-Magic:	55
Anti-Fire:	59
Load (Kg):	38

STATS

Class: Fighter
Level: Novice

Swing:	0
Thrust:	0
Club:	0
Parry:	4

Class: Priest
Level: Apprentice

Identify:	3
Heal:	5
Influence:	3
Defend:	2

Class: Ninja
Level: Tyro

Fight:	0
Throw:	0
Shoot:	0

Class: Wizard
Level: Neophyte

Fire:	0
Air:	0
Earth:	2
Water:	2

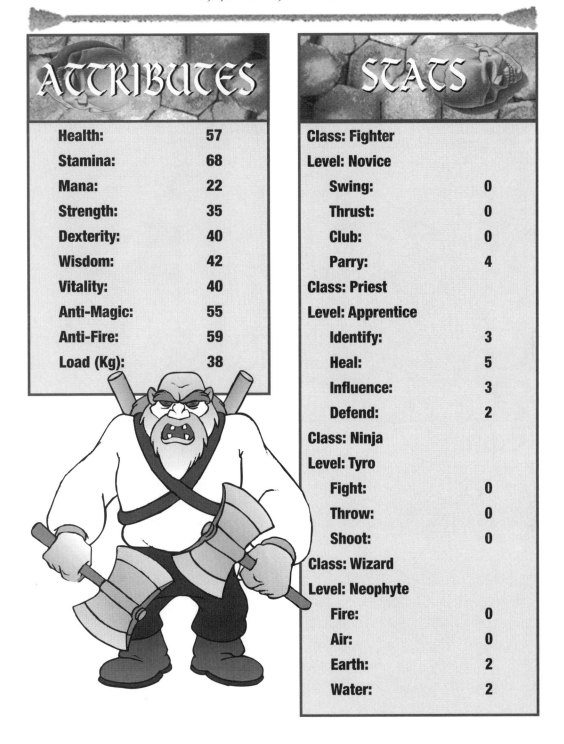

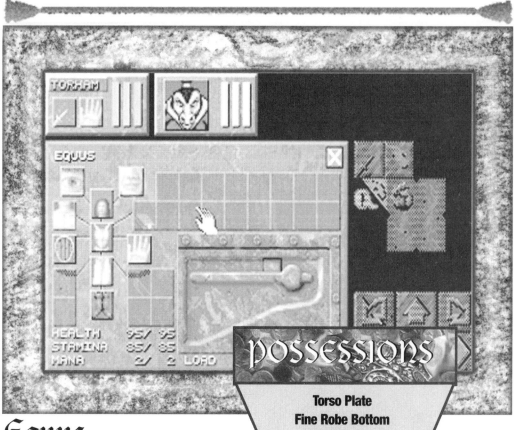

Equus

 Due to his ancestry, he comes battle-ready in full armor and lacking only in dexterity, which can be remedied by developing Ninja skills. Mana development will be a tough monster to slay.

POSSESSIONS

Torso Plate
Fine Robe Bottom
Black Boots
Wood Shield
Money Box
with 1 Silver Coin
2 Copper Coins
2 Gold Coins

ATTRIBUTES

Health:	95
Stamina:	85
Mana:	2
Strength:	58
Dexterity:	30
Wisdom:	36
Vitality:	50
Anti-Magic:	30
Anti-Fire:	32
Load (Kg):	57

STATS

Class: Fighter
Level: Neophyte

Swing:	0
Thrust:	0
Club:	2
Parry:	3

Class: Priest
Level: Tyro

Identify:	0
Heal:	0
Influence:	0
Defend:	2

Class: Ninja
Level: Apprentice

Fight:	5
Throw:	0
Shoot:	0

Class: Wizard
Level: Tyro

Fire:	0
Air:	0
Earth:	1
Water:	0

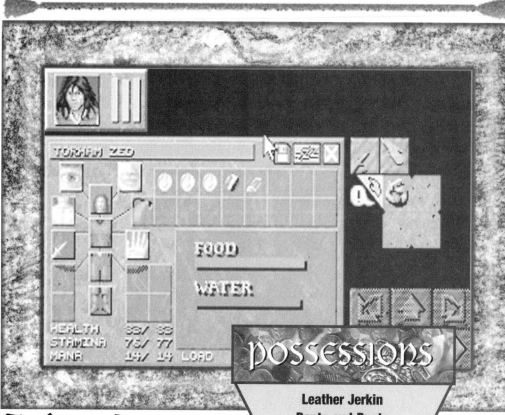

Torham Zed

Obviously, you know a little about yourself. But let me just say that you are the best adventurer of the lot, as far as general use goes. And might I also add that such a generous gentleman as yourself is sure to go far in the world. Barkeep!

POSSESSIONS

Leather Jerkin
Pants and Boots
Dagger
Bota
Green Gem
1 Silver Coin
3 Gold Coins

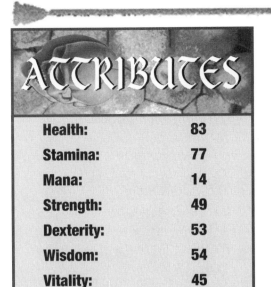

ATTRIBUTES

Health:	83
Stamina:	77
Mana:	14
Strength:	49
Dexterity:	53
Wisdom:	54
Vitality:	45
Anti-Magic:	30
Anti-Fire:	38
Load (Kg):	50

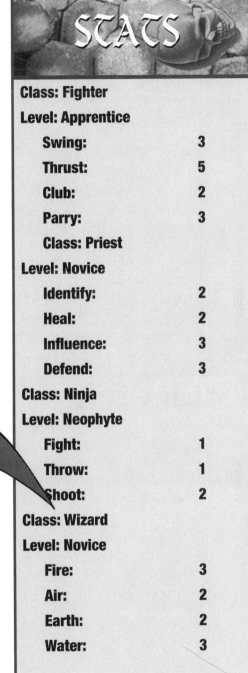

STATS

Class: Fighter
Level: Apprentice

Swing:	3
Thrust:	5
Club:	2
Parry:	3

Class: Priest
Level: Novice

Identify:	2
Heal:	2
Influence:	3
Defend:	3

Class: Ninja
Level: Neophyte

Fight:	1
Throw:	1
Shoot:	2

Class: Wizard
Level: Novice

Fire:	3
Air:	2
Earth:	2
Water:	3

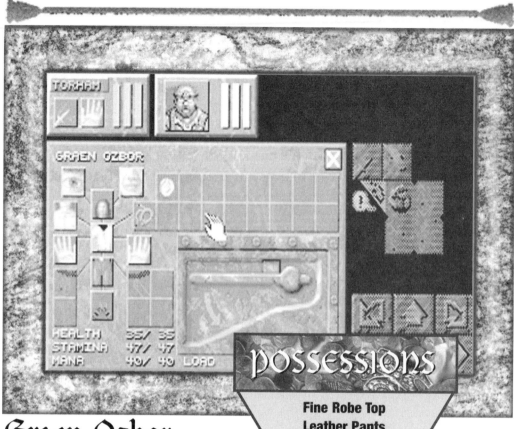

Graen Ozbor

Graen is the best of the lot as far as mage and clerical abilities go. You won't need much work on the steel with this one; his arsenal will be primarily magickal in nature. Notice he also has a most unique and useful item: rope. You will want to protect this one well.

POSSESSIONS

Fine Robe Top
Leather Pants
Sandals
Rope
1 Gold Coin

ATTRIBUTES

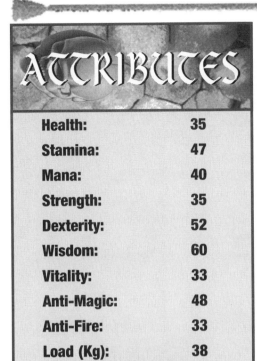

Health:	35
Stamina:	47
Mana:	40
Strength:	35
Dexterity:	52
Wisdom:	60
Vitality:	33
Anti-Magic:	48
Anti-Fire:	33
Load (Kg):	38

STATS

Class: Fighter
Level: Tyro

Swing:	0
Thrust:	0
Club:	0
Parry:	0

Class: Priest
Level: Novice

Identify:	4
Heal:	0
Influence:	0
Defend:	0

Class: Ninja
Level: Neophyte

Fight:	0
Throw:	0
Shoot:	3

Class: Wizard
Level: Apprentice

Fire:	4
Air:	3
Earth:	4
Water:	3

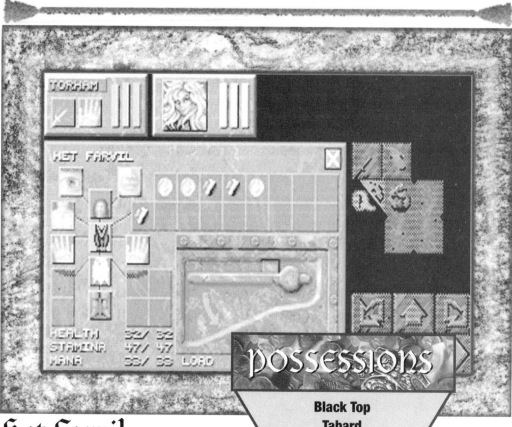

Het Farvil

Het isn't much of fighter, but her spell-casting potential is great. Placed in the back and given practice with spells, she will quickly become a formidable healer and sorceress.

POSSESSIONS

Black Top
Tabard
Leather Boots
3 Gold Coins
3 Silver Coins

ATTRIBUTES

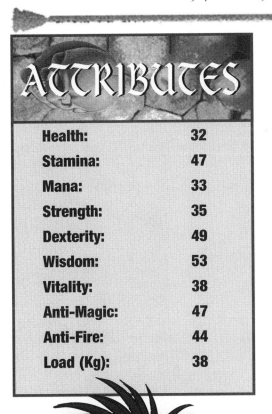

Health:	32
Stamina:	47
Mana:	33
Strength:	35
Dexterity:	49
Wisdom:	53
Vitality:	38
Anti-Magic:	47
Anti-Fire:	44
Load (Kg):	38

STATS

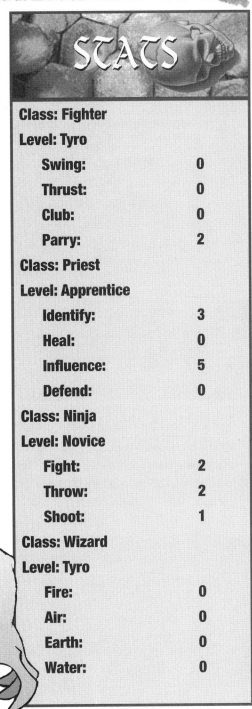

Class: Fighter
Level: Tyro

Swing:	0
Thrust:	0
Club:	0
Parry:	2

Class: Priest
Level: Apprentice

Identify:	3
Heal:	0
Influence:	5
Defend:	0

Class: Ninja
Level: Novice

Fight:	2
Throw:	2
Shoot:	1

Class: Wizard
Level: Tyro

Fire:	0
Air:	0
Earth:	0
Water:	0

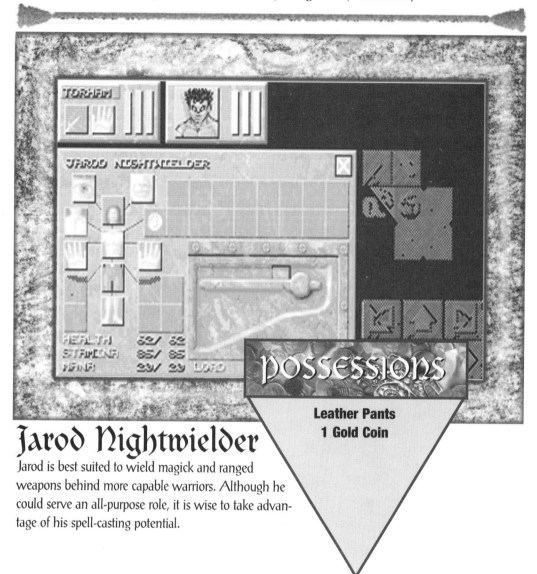

Jarod Nightwielder

Jarod is best suited to wield magick and ranged weapons behind more capable warriors. Although he could serve an all-purpose role, it is wise to take advantage of his spell-casting potential.

possessions

Leather Pants
1 Gold Coin

ATTRIBUTES

Health:	62
Stamina:	85
Mana:	20
Strength:	37
Dexterity:	59
Wisdom:	52
Vitality:	40
Anti-Magic:	52
Anti-Fire:	33
Load (Kg):	40

STATS

Class: Fighter
Level: Tyro

Swing:	0
Thrust:	0
Club:	0
Parry:	0

Class: Priest
Level: Tyro

Identify:	0
Heal:	0
Influence:	0
Defend:	0

Class: Ninja
Level: Novice

Fight:	4
Throw:	3
Shoot:	2

Class: Wizard
Level: Apprentice

Fire:	2
Air:	3
Earth:	4
Water:	2

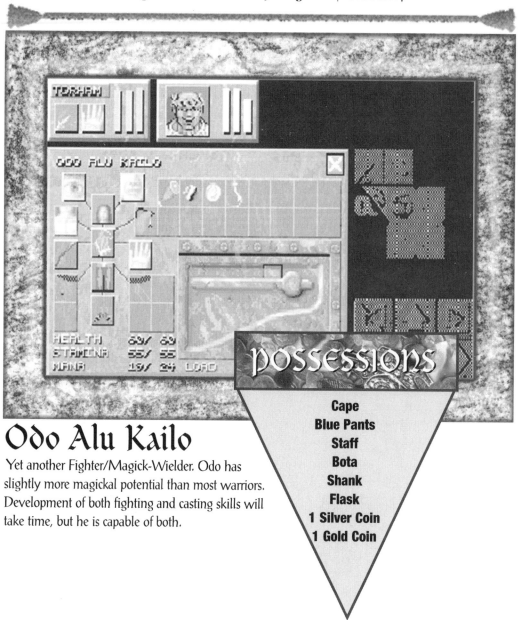

Odo Alu Kailo

Yet another Fighter/Magick-Wielder. Odo has slightly more magickal potential than most warriors. Development of both fighting and casting skills will take time, but he is capable of both.

POSSESSIONS

Cape
Blue Pants
Staff
Bota
Shank
Flask
1 Silver Coin
1 Gold Coin

ATTRIBUTES

Health:	60
Stamina:	55
Mana:	19
Strength:	55
Dexterity:	30
Wisdom:	41
Vitality:	44
Anti-Magic:	35
Anti-Fire:	40
Load (Kg):	54

STATS

Class: Fighter	
Level: Novice	
Swing:	3
Thrust:	0
Club:	4
Parry:	0
Class: Priest	
Level: Apprentice	
Identify:	2
Heal:	5
Influence:	4
Defend:	2
Class: Ninja	
Level: Tyro	
Fight:	0
Throw:	0
Shoot:	0
Class: Wizard	
Level: Tyro	
Fire:	0
Air:	0
Earth:	0
Water:	0

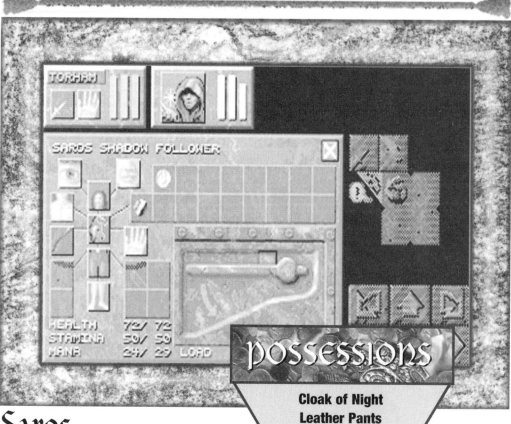

Saros, Shadow Follower

Saros is reminiscent of Graen, although his skill may not increase as quickly. He begins as a capable mage and has great potential as a Priest, also. Place him behind warriors and develop his magickal potential.

POSSESSIONS

Cloak of Night
Leather Pants
Staff
1 Gold Coin
1 Silver Coin

ATTRIBUTES

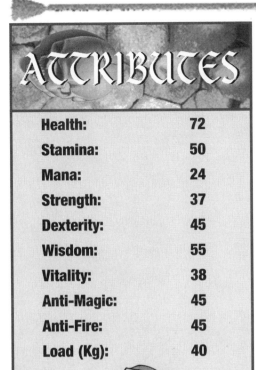

Health:	72
Stamina:	50
Mana:	24
Strength:	37
Dexterity:	45
Wisdom:	55
Vitality:	38
Anti-Magic:	45
Anti-Fire:	45
Load (Kg):	40

STATS

Class: Fighter	
Level: Tyro	
Swing:	0
Thrust:	0
Club:	0
Parry:	0
Class: Priest	
Level: Neophyte	
Identify:	1
Heal:	3
Influence:	0
Defend:	2
Class: Ninja	
Level: Tyro	
Fight:	0
Throw:	0
Shoot:	0
Class: Wizard	
Level: Journeyman	
Fire:	3
Air:	3
Earth:	5
Water:	5

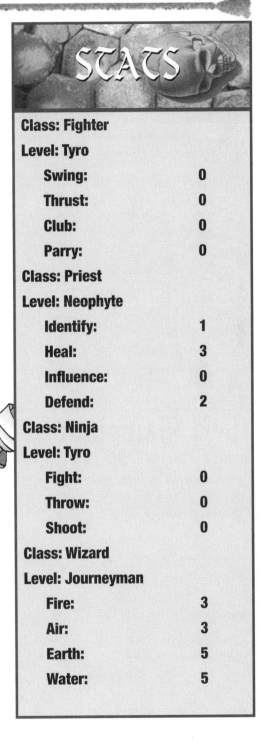

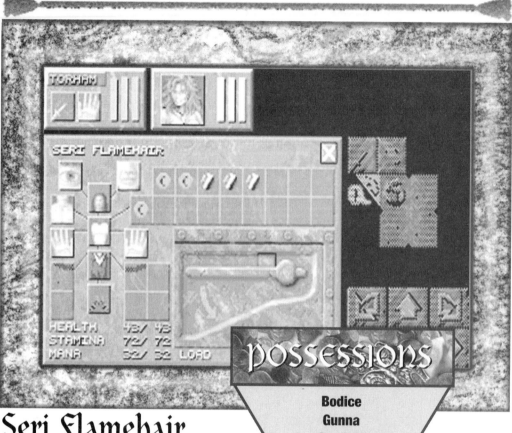

Seri Flamehair

Seri is not much of a fighter but is quite capable of mana specialization. She comes complete with advanced clerical skill and high natural resistance to magick and flame.

POSSESSIONS

Bodice
Gunna
Sandals
3 Copper Coins
3 Silver Coins

ATTRIBUTES

Health:	43
Stamina:	72
Mana:	32
Strength:	30
Dexterity:	46
Wisdom:	51
Vitality:	45
Anti-Magic:	42
Anti-Fire:	50
Load (Kg):	34

STATS

Class: Fighter
Level: Tyro

Swing:	0
Thrust:	0
Club:	0
Parry:	0

Class: Priest
Level: Journeyman

Identify:	3
Heal:	5
Influence:	6
Defend:	3

Class: Ninja
Level: Tyro

Fight:	0
Throw:	0
Shoot:	0

Class: Wizard
Level: Neophyte

Fire:	0
Air:	3
Earth:	2
Water:	1

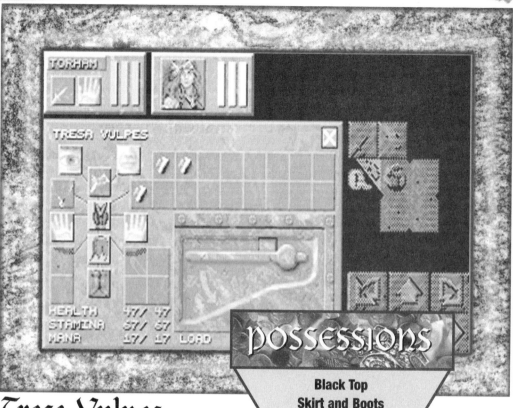

Tresa Vulpes

Tresa is capable of both fighting and spell-casting;
however becoming proficient will require practice. She
needs protection during this process but will become a
well-rounded heroine.

POSSESSIONS

**Black Top
Skirt and Boots
Bandanna
Jewel of Symal
3 Silver Coins**

ATTRIBUTES

Health:	47
Stamina:	67
Mana:	17
Strength:	47
Dexterity:	54
Wisdom:	42
Vitality:	31
Anti-Magic:	35
Anti-Fire:	47
Load (Kg):	48

STATS

Class: Fighter
Level: Tyro

Swing:	0
Thrust:	0
Club:	0
Parry:	0

Class: Priest
Level: Tyro

Identify:	0
Heal:	0
Influence:	0
Defend:	0

Class: Ninja
Level: Apprentice

Fight:	4
Throw:	0
Shoot:	5

Class: Wizard
Level: Novice

Fire:	3
Air:	3
Earth:	2
Water:	2

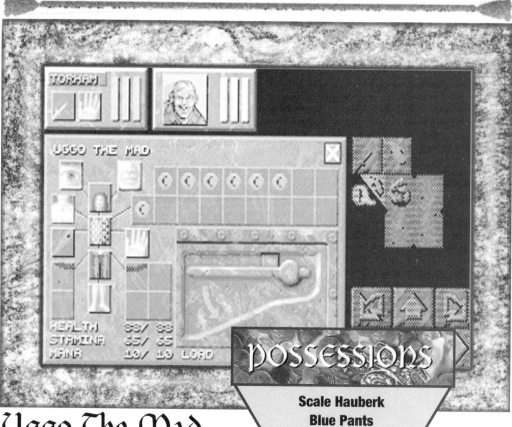

Uggo The Mad

Not even Uggo is sure what his role in life is. Most likely a fighter, he can also grudgingly work with magick, but his strong natural resistance to it suggests that he would rather not.

POSSESSIONS

Scale Hauberk
Blue Pants
Club
7 Copper Coins

ATTRIBUTES

Health:	88
Stamina:	65
Mana:	10
Strength:	55
Dexterity:	37
Wisdom:	30
Vitality:	47
Anti-Magic:	52
Anti-Fire:	30
Load (Kg):	54

STATS

Class: Fighter
Level: Apprentice

Swing:	3
Thrust:	0
Club:	5
Parry:	1

Class: Priest
Level: Tyro

Identify:	0
Heal:	0
Influence:	0
Defend:	0

Class: Ninja
Level: Novice

Fight:	4
Throw:	1
Shoot:	0

Class: Wizard
Level: Neophyte

Fire:	1
Air:	3
Earth:	0
Water:	0

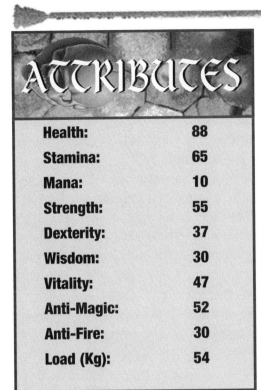

Achieving Balance: The Perfect Party

When choosing your party members, take note of their initial stats, which tell you not only whether they are best suited for steel or sorcery, but how quickly those skills can be advanced. Obvious fighter-types are capable of learning and using mana skills, but the process takes much longer than it will for those with high wisdom and mana already. Likewise, spell-casters gain adequate fighting ability with time if you put them in front to melee, but getting them proficient with heavy weapons takes much longer, and increases the risk of untimely death.

The best strategy is to choose adventurers already advanced in or with stats that favor one of the four classes, then spend time developing other skills to a passable level so that you don't get caught with inadequate fighting or spell-casting abilities if one (or more) of your members dies. Developing skills also raises primary stats (Hit Points, Stamina, Mana) and applicable attributes (Wisdom for spells, Strength for fighting, etc.) much faster than just concentrating on improving the hero's main class.

The reason is simple: The more progress you make, the harder it is to improve. However, when you are at the bottom of a class, progress can be quite rapid. And each time you progress, you raise your statistics. Hence, working at something you are already well-versed in will provide gains only over time. But concentrating at first on bringing up a hero's deficient classes, just by a couple of levels, will improve stats much more rapidly.

Ideally, all four adventurers in your party will be capable of any given melee or sorcerer's task to at least a minor degree, while still having one highly specialized advanced ability.

So, there isn't one "best party." If you really wished to, you could complete your fate with just you and Graen Ozbor alone, although it would be a Herculean task. But some fighters and mages tend to work together better than others in the initial stages of the game, before everyone has had the time to develop their full skills. Graen Ozbor; Equus; Bane, Blade Cleaver; and you make a particularly good match.

However, don't feel restricted. If you are partial to another hero, feel free to select them. But try to always balance magic and might in your selections.

Dressing For Success: An Introduction to Armor and Weapons

Unless you select champions who already have good equipment, good armor and weapons are hard to come by until at least the third quest. They can't be found lying around, and the shop prices are prohibitively high.

The little money allotted to the party is best spent right away on armor, though it will not get you much. The most important item the party can afford is the Tech Helm available in the local shop. While there is only one of these items, it is worth its weight. When worn, the Tech Helm will raise the wisdom of the wearer 20 points, making even a dumb fighter capable of learning spells much faster and greatly enhancing a specialized spell-caster's abilities.

The most important thing to know about armor at the start of your journey is that it needs to be worn by those in front. The two front party members are going to be the ones receiving the most damage. Hence, they always need to be armored as much as possible, even when at the expense of the two rear members.

Weapons aren't nearly as important as armor since all of your heroes come conveniently equipped with hands and feet (I should have had it so easy). In fact, learning to fight unarmed will quickly raise the Ninja skill, which is more important in the starting stages of your journey than fighter ability, since it advances Dexterity and will improve your dodging and accuracy.

You will find that killing your foes with hands and feet takes more time and effort, but the rewards are faster skill advancement and higher statistics.

A Note On Marching Order

Marching order is very simple, but it is also critical to get it right. Fighters go in front, spell-casters and archers behind them. Although you are going to move people around a bit to develop abilities, this is the basic pattern you want.

While developing all the characters in the party is important, it is also necessary to remember the brutal fact that those with the Hit Points survive combat better and travel in front most often.

Fundamental Principles of Combat

The rule of combat I like best is "when in doubt, run away." It has always worked for me, and I see no need to change it. Oh, yea verily, there are those who would heap disparaging comments on me for such an attitude, but I think it wise to always keep the idea of retreat foremost in my mind.

Look closely at the wrinkles in my eyes, my well developed ale-gut; these things are the signs of an old adventurer. If you want to get to be an old adventurer, you learn to run away whenever the opportunity presents itself.

You see, monsters don't rest well. Their insomnia is caused by all the evil deeds they commit or some such problem. They just can't get a good night's sleep. Now, I don't sleep so well, either, but that is due to the gout, another matter entirely.

So you attack the enemy, drain them down a bit and then, in the tradition of great cowards everywhere, run away. Don't let your pride stop you. Turn tail and run. The monsters, instead of tending to their physical wounds, will have a great party over their victory and generally drink too much and have wrestling contests and all the silly things monsters do when they think they have won a battle.

You, on the other hand, get a good night's sleep. In the morning you will feel much better. And the monsters! They will all be mean and hung over, and generally won't feel any better than when you left them. Go back and wipe up the ground with them. All those yokels who were taunting you with catcalls the night before will think twice when you come into town the next day with a few demon skulls adorning your armor.

Death and Other Minor Annoyances

Adventuring, being a wet, cold, and generally disagreeable occupation, is full of annoyances. One of the biggest is dying. While it isn't quite as annoying as cracklebugs in your boots, it is much more vexing than, say, cold rations. Hence, it is a good thing for you and your party members to avoid until you are forced into it. The good news is that all party members can be resurected as long as at least one party member survives.

Not to say that it is a big problem. While I convinced my party leader, Tanic, that it was only through my great magickal powers that the members of the party could be resurrected on the altar near the sleeping chambers, the real fact of the matter is that if you lay the remains of any dead party member on the altar; biff, bang, boom — there they are, back up and around as if nothing happened. Then they have to take that unmerciful ribbing from everyone else in the party. You know the kind of thing, "Oh, pretty spry for a dead guy," or, "Well, sleeping beauty's up and around again, is he!" That sort of abuse.

Nobody likes to take that. You don't start adventuring to look like a goof who can't even stay in one piece do you? No, of course not. You adventure to look good, get the girls, and all that. And, more of a problem, once you have made some progress, it gets to be a real drag hauling back some dead carcass halfway across the realm to get resurrected.

The moral of the story? Watch your party carefully for damage, and avoid a fight when some of your members are near death. Give them time to heal. That way, you don't have to hike back, and they don't have to worry about getting all the abuse from their mates and looking bad.

Well, that about wraps it up for this bit. Next I am going to tell you a little about what to expect right out of the gate, in the first area outside of the sleeping chambers.

Barkeep! Look at this poor man! He is positively parched and famished. I think you should bring him some food and more ale. Just draw off a pitcher while you're there; I think he is going to need it before the night is out.

An important factor for the player in effectively guiding Torham and his party around the world of Dungeon Master II is familiarity with the interface and whatever pointing device is being used. It takes practice to click on the right icons quickly.

When using melee weapons, the two front-line fighters have an advantage in speed over the two in the rear due to the placement of the action icons.

When you click on the bottom edge of the icon it will produce a pulldown menu of the attack choices for that particular weapon. Notice that the pointer is already at the top edge of the first choice on the menu for that weapon. Thus, just clicking a second time selects and launches a punch. Holding the pointer in this position and clicking repeatedly executes many punches rapidly. This works for any of the four action icons carried by the front two party members, but is only effective for that first choice on the menu.

The more powerful attacks, which come further down on the menu, will suffer from a time disadvantage, since the pointer must be moved down to activate these functions.

Fight with open hands using the repeated clicking technique near the beginning of the game to create rapid attacks and raise the important Ninja skills at the same time.

Recruiting
A Groovy War Band

h, yes, those first moments out on the adventure. I remember them well. Tanic had just awakened me, as I explained earlier, and we were about to get Zilch and Ravenblood, our fighter and our cleric, respectively.

Zilch was our first recruit. He was a great, blond, muscular, dimwit of a man. Absolutely huge. And he said next to nothing.

I am not really sure whether he was as dim before we tried to wake him up, however.

Looking in the sarcophagus, we could see he was just the kind of fighter we needed.

"Look at him, will you? Simply huge! Just the kind of man for this sort of work," said Tanic.

"Well, pop the lid and talk him into it," I said while nursing a rip in my cloak Tanic had made when wrestling me back into the room from my attempted break for the pub.

Tanic reached down to the lid and started to pry. He just kept prying until finally, he gave it a mighty heave with all his might, and — right before I thought his eyes were going to pop out — he simply let go and stepped back from it, glaring.

"Stuck."

"Oh well, time to give up the whole thing and head for the pub, I guess," I said as I started for the door.

Tanic pulled out a dagger and started doing his nails in a most threatening manner.

"You're the wizard. Cast a spell on it," he said.

I looked at him with my best haughty expression.

"I don't do doors."

"Well, then," he said with something that was not quite a leer on his face. "I guess you and I will just march side by side the whole way."

I looked in the sarcophagus again. This Zilch fellow certainly was the sort of chap built just for a sorcerer to hide behind.

"I have a plan," I said.

I reached into my bag and pulled out a large magnifying lens that I used to read some of the more scrawled incantations in older grimores. I held it up over the viewport of the sarcophagus, and stuck my mouth up to it, showing my teeth and gnashing them a bit. Then I banged on the side of the stone coffin with a rock.

Zilch's eyes opened, then he screamed and hammered his fists into the lid, which flew up, slammed me in the face, and fell back down. Of course, Zilch was trying to sit up to defend himself and the rebounding lid met his head as he was trying to sit up. The lid shattered and he went out cold.

"Well, you got it unstuck," said Tanic.

He opened it up and, after a bit of work, managed to bring Zilch around. I was using my robe to stop the blood from my busted lip.

Tanic tried to explain things to Zilch, who didn't seem to be getting much of it. He just got up and wandered around the chamber, rubbing his eyes and his head alternately and mumbling about great fanged monsters.

Then there was Ravenblood, who seemed downright annoyed from the moment we awakened him.

"Sleeping, you fool," he mumbled, reaching up to pull his sarcophagus shut.

Tanic stopped the lid from shutting by quickly sticking the hilt of his dagger in the hinge.

"Uh, but we have to save the world, from Dragoth. The demon, you see. . . ."

"What we really have to do is get a pint or two of ale," I muttered under my breath.

Tanic stared death at me while struggling to keep Ravenblood from removing the wedged dagger from the hinge.

"Leave me out of it," he said. "I don't want to get involved. Trying to sleep. So sorry. Catch me when I wake up."

Ravenblood kicked the dagger and almost got the lid down, but at the last second Tanic did a cross-body block-type tricky fighter number, wedged his shoulder onto the edge of the descending lid, and muscled it open.

"This isn't a trivial matter," Tanic said. "Dragoth will lay the world to waste."

"As long he lays you to waste, then I can get some sleep," muttered Ravenblood, trying to turn over in his sarcophagus to avoid the intruding light.

I waved Tanic off and leaned in close to Ravenblood.

"Uh, you know, Magic User to Magic User, I'm not too keen on the whole idea myself."

"Then why don't you sod off like a good hero and let me go to sleep then, eh!" Ravenblood fluffed his pillow.

"I would, you know, but then I would feel responsible for what would happen to you."

This got his attention. He looked around at me.

"For what would happen to me!"

"Yea, verily. I would feel like I hadn't warned you."

He looked slightly nervous.

"Warned me about what!"

"You see that great monster of a man!" I pointed at Zilch.

He nodded.

"I tried to go back to sleep," I pointed at Zilch's shattered sarcophagus, "and he went insane. Just hammered through the lid and pulled me out."

I showed him the blood on my ripped robes and pointed to my lip.

"I agreed to the whole idea quickly and got away with only this. Lucky, I'd say. Just look at the size of him. Hammered straight through that rock lid with just his bare hands."

Ravenblood looked at Zilch and rapidly got out of his sleeping casket.

"Say, I think saving the world sounds, well, rather like a duty, don't you think!" Ravenblood said.

Tanic looked at him and smiled widely.

"Glad to have you aboard."

From there, it was up the ladder into the main building. The initial room was dim and dank and filled with a bric-a-brac well as a large altar.

"There might be something here we need," said Tanic. "Search the place."

I ignored him and walked over to inspect the altar. Nice, as such things go.

A scroll sat on the altar. I picked it up and examined it. My eyes almost bugged out and I let out a low whistle.

The scroll explained that this was an altar of resurrection. Simply place a dead body on it, and it would come back to life. Now, that was just the sort of thing an able-bodied adventurer needed. I suddenly felt a lot better about this whole hero business.

I turned to tell everyone about my find but thought better of it and stuffed the scroll in my pocket.

Everyone was messing with a picture on the wall. I grabbed a staff laying about and leaned heavily on it. Getting up from sleep to save the world is one thing. Working hard while doing it is another.

Rapidly they finished trashing the room. Pretty shady for heroes, in my opinion. Tanic might be all full of good intentions but didn't think twice about grabbing everything that wasn't nailed down. Not that I have a problem with taking most anything that isn't properly protected, mind you. I am just a bit more up front about it.

Finally we clustered up near the door and headed out.

Tanic jumped backwards as soon as the door was opened.

"By Zorin's eyes!" he exclaimed.

In the courtyard was a gelatinous mass.

"What's that, I wonder?" I asked Ravenblood casually, as the mass began to devour Tanic's foot.

Ravenblood leaned against a low table.

"Darned if I know, but it looks like they have it under control, don't you think?"

At this point the creature had consumed about half of Tanic's leg and was working it's way up as Tanic frantically beat on it with his fists.

"Oh, verily," I agreed. "Tanic and Zilch are quite the professionals, aren't they?. We'd just get in the way up there."

I watched how fast the thing appeared to move and judged my distance to the ladder down to the sleeping chamber. If it finished with Tanic, I would have plenty of time to get down the ladder.

Tanic continued to pound on the thing rather ineffectively. Finally, Zilch looked down at it and gave a mighty kick. The thing died promptly, spitting out Tanic's leg as it did so.

Shaken, Tanic examined his leg. It was cut here and there, but he could still walk on it without a major limp. He and Zilch proceeded out the door.

I followed — not out of a great sense of need to meet more nasty creatures but mainly because the nearest pub was in the direction of the courtyard.

There was a bit more moshing of creatures in the courtyard, but finally Zilch and Tanic managed to get them all squared away. I started straight for the pub.

"Where do you think you're going?" said Tanic, noting my definite tilt toward the pub.

"Well, I was rather thinking, we should head for the pub you know, get a bite maybe," I said. "I'm absolutely famished. All sleep and no food makes Alran a nasty wizard."

Tanic looked at me skeptically. You would think I had "Sot" stitched on my robes.

"I think we'd best get started right off," he said. "We can find food on the trail."

"Hungry," said Zilch in a rumbling bass, and he started toward the door of the pub. I smiled angelically at Tanic.

In the pub, I immediately downed a few pints in rapid gulps to fortify myself for some serious drinking. Then I got a pitcher and left the bar. By the time I got back, Tanic and Ravenblood were talking to a grizzled old man seated in the corner. Zilch was in the general vicinity, but his interest was limited solely to the thorn demon steak he was devouring with loud chomps.

"The keys to the whole matter," wheezed the old man as I walked up and set my pitcher on the table, "are the magickal maps. Just what you need, those. While they only cover a short distance around you, it is much better to have a magickal map than to just stumble into danger unaware."

> **BE SURE TO GET ALL THE MAGICKAL MAPS AND MAKE USE OF THEM. THE FIRST ONE WILL SHOW YOUR IMMEDIATE AREA, THE NEXT WILL SHOW THE LOCATION OF MONSTERS, MISSILES, TRAPS, AND SECRET DOORS. THE FINAL TWO MAPS WILL PROVIDE SUMMONED MINIONS: ONE TO SCOUT FOR THE PARTY AND THE OTHER TO FETCH AND CARRY OBJECTS. THE MAGICK MARKERS ARE ALSO MUCH EASIER TO FOLLOW WITH THESE MAPS.**

I surfaced from my ale.

"Magickal Maps, eh. How do they work, and how much do you want for one?" I wasn't some country bumpkin. I knew a pub hustler when I heard one.

"Oh, you have to find them, but there is no cost involved," he replied. " The last time I checked, there was one in the hall. No one has needed it for quite some time, not much call for adventuring types before this current problem."

"To use it is quite easy; you simply open it and look at it. It will show you the area right around the map. It takes a tiny amount of your magickal energy to keep it running, but it will show you the outlines of the area around you." He stopped and took a small sip from the glass of water on the table.

"The next map, however, is quite some way from here, near the lightning altar, but it is much more powerful. This map is activated simply by gazing upon it and touching one of the four magical enhancement icons across the bottom. The first, KU, shows the position of all other creatures in the map area. The second, ROS, shows false walls and traps or niches. The third, DAIN, shows any missile weapons and whether they are in flight or lying on the ground. The fourth, NETA, causes the map to freeze where you are currently at. In that way, you can observe what happens in a place even when you go away from it."

I drank a bit and watched Zilch stuff another handful of food into the small cavern that passed for his mouth.

"But the Minion maps are even more powerful," the old seer went on. "The Moon Altar has the Scout Map. This map allows the user to create a scout minion in the spot where the party is standing. Then the user can select another spot on the map and the minion will travel to that point, the map following along. In this way, the wielders of the map can explore areas without traveling to them."

We needed that map. Then we could select the spot on the map that corresponded with Zilch's stomach and see a minion point of view of Zilch's entrails.

"The scout minion is limited to only those places, however, that would normally be accessible on foot."

So much for the idea of mapping Zilch's insides with it.

"It cannot go through closed doors or the like. It can change levels, if you mark the spot with a ladder or stairway on the map twice in rapid succession, but that is all. When finished with the minion, simply press the minion rune again and the minion will dissipate. The map will center on the party once again."

"The final map, the Fetch/Carry Minion map, is the most powerful of all in its subtle way. This map summons a fetch- or carry-minion to move things. To use this, simply draw an "x" on the map at the position you wish to have something carried from or to. Then press the appropriate icon, and whatever is at that location will be carried to you, or whatever is with you now will be carried to that location. Remember, however, that you must be at the location where you want the "x" to be marked. And if you re-mark another location, the first one will be erased."

"You mean that we have to go somewhere, mark the map, after which we will be able to recall items to or from that place!"
asked Tanic.

"Exactly."

"So what's the point, if we are already there!"

"I can see one use right away: putting an "x" near our resurrection altar. That way, if someone falls in combat, we can get the minion to transport them to the altar, and not have to deal with going back ourselves." I said.

"Resurrection altar?" said Tanic, looking bewildered.

"Yes, as everyone knows — umph!" the old man's sentence was abruptly cut off as I brutally kicked his shin under the table.

"As everyone knows, I have the power to bring people back from the dead," I said casually, polishing my fingernails idly on a loose fold of my cloak.

"Oh, yes, and pigs can fly."

I looked at him earnestly.

"With the right spells."

"You can't really. . ."

"Special arrangement with the powers that be. I have the resurrection concession for the entire area. I put a quick mark on the deceased's remains, put them on the altar, and — poof, spontaneous generation. Live flesh from dead and all that."

"You jest."

"Ask him," I casually waved a hand at the sage. As soon as Tanic turned towards him I gave the sage one of my most powerful evil glowers, making it obvious his fate would be none too pleasant if he told Tanic that anyone could resurrect people with the right altar.

The sage fidgeted. Sages are notorious about telling the truth. A serious sage character flaw in my opinion. I cranked up the glower a notch and started reaching for my rune bag.

"Yes, if he lays a dead body on the altar, it will come back to life," he said.

The sage, within the strict definition, had told the truth, but he still looked a little dodgy. I bared my teeth at him. And, as Tanic twisted back to me, turned the corners of my mouth enough to make the expression into a bored smile.

"Enough about me," I said, fearing that Ravenblood would burst out into guffaws of laughter, as he looked about to do gazing at Tanic's awed expression. "Are there any limits on the powers of the Fetch/Carry Minion map?"

"Well, yes. They aren't all that bright. Hence they can't make it through a very complicated path or one that is blocked. So it doesn't work as well inside the keep. It can also be canceled in its flight, but that will cause it to drop everything it is carrying wherever it dissipates."

He took another drink of water.

We all sat and stared at each other for a few moments and then jumped, startled by a loud bang from Zilch's side of the table.

He had passed out cold from his great meal. His head had slammed down right beside his plate, and he was snoring peacefully. Never a man to see ale go to waste, I took his cup and drained it handily.

"Ah, the side effects of a good meal," laughed Ravenblood.

"You know that does bring up a point I was meaning to mention," I said. "Being something of a city dweller, I am wondering just how we are going to come by food on our little adventure?"

Tanic snorted.

"Digger worms."

"Is that the name of a chain of path-side pubs?"

"No. Digger worms, annoying little creatures that are quite edible. You find them out in the wild."

I just stared at him.

"Quite tasty really, once you get over the slime and all."

"Surely you jest."

"Well, they aren't all that filling, but you have to make do out in the wild."

"No, you have to make do out in the wild. If you think I am going to be eating worms, we have a real problem with this whole undertaking."

"But they keep you from starving to death," he said.

I just snorted.

"Well, there are the thorn demon steaks."

"Yes, available at any good pub."

"Or from thorn demons, though they are a bit hard to kill."

"You mean, thorn demons out in the wild? Aren't there domesticated thorn demons!"

"No, they are all rather nasty creatures. Why do you think thorn demon steak costs so much?"

I mulled it over. It did make sort of good sense.

"Are these wild thorn demon steaks as good as the ones here in the pub?"

"Oh, even better, from a taste point of view. Fresher. And quite filling. A couple will take care of a person who is even at the edge of starvation."

I thought about it.

"Well, I like thorn demon enough, when it's marinated well. I guess I wouldn't mind eating them."

"Yes, well, leave plenty of space in your pack for thorn demon steaks. There won't be that many herds of them between here and Dragoth."

KILLING A DIGGER WORM PROVIDES THE PARTY WITH THREE TO FOUR WORM ROUNDS, WHICH ARE EDIBLE, BUT DON'T GO AS FAR AS THEY SHOULD TO FEED FOUR HUNGRY MOUTHS. THE BEST SOURCE OF FOOD IS THORN DEMONS, FOUND NEAR THE LIGHTNING ALTAR. WHILE QUITE HARD TO KILL, EACH CREATURE PROVIDES THREE OR FOUR THORN DEMON STEAKS, AND EVEN A STARVING ADVENTURER WILL BE COMPLETELY STUFFED AFTER ONLY TWO OF THEM. IT IS A GOOD IDEA TO STOCK UP ON THEM AT EVERY OPPORTUNITY TO KEEP FROM HAVING TO CONSTANTLY TREK BACK TO TOWN FOR MORE FOOD.

We adjourned at that point to the courtyard. Not before, of course I had filled my bota with some fine ale.

"So what do we do now?"

"Well, let's see what they have in the shops."

So we spent a good part of the afternoon shopping. I wasn't particularly interested in the whole process, so I took every opportunity I could to duck back to the pub for a quick one. By the time we were done we had a helmet that magickally raised the wisdom of the wearer, some armor, and a wonderful black cloak that flowed quite well.

> WHEN CHOOSING NEW EQUIPMENT WITH WHAT LITTLE MONEY THE PARTY HAS IN THE OPENING STAGES OF THE ADVENTURE, THE BEST BUYS ARE TECH HELM, TECH PLATE, CLOAK OF NIGHT, TWO POISON DARTS, AND THE SWORD. ANYTHING MORE EXPENSIVE IS NICE BUT LIKELY NOT WORTH THE SACRIFICE. NUMEROUS LOW-PRICED, HIGH QUALITY ITEMS ARE AVAILABLE FOR YOU TO OUTFIT THE WHOLE PARTY INSTEAD OF TOTALLY OUTFITTING ONE INDIVIDUAL. THE BEST STRATEGY IS TO TRY TO RELY ON SPELLS AND ANY AVAILABLE WEAPONS UNTIL THE PARTY COMES ACROSS MORE CASH (DURING THE FOURTH AND FIFTH QUEST SEGMENTS OF YOUR ADVENTURING).

"Well, that's that. Let's be off then," said Tanic happily, as he started off smartly for the door eager to leave town.

Ravenblood and I looked at each other earnestly.

"Er, I don't think that would be too wise," said Ravenblood. Sometimes you just have to love your fellow back row hero, and this was one of those times.

Tanic turned.

"And why's that," he asked with hands on hips.

"Er, well there are all sorts of nasty beasts out there and — ," he paused, trying to think of a stalling maneuver.

"We need to practice," I filled in smoothly. "I mean, what if something should happen to one of us! We should spend some time here now that we have secured the area in a most heroic fashion."

Tanic glowed a bit with pride on that one.

"And use it to work up to this thing, cross-training and all that," I finished rather lamely, I thought.

Tanic considered it for a second.

"Nope." He turned and started marching for the door again. I gave Ravenblood a 'well, we tried' shrug.

And once again, Zilch came to our rescue.

"Tired," he said, as he sat down against a wall and promptly fell asleep. That man was very serious about his sleep.

"Well, that would be that then," I said, tapping Ravenblood on the shoulder and starting back for the pub.

"Stop," Tanic ominously rumbled. "You said we needed to train. We train."

"Well, maybe we should talk over our training plan. In the pub, that is . . ."

"We train," said Tanic, passing me two darts he had bought in the shop and pointing to a thick wooden door nearby.

I looked at the darts skeptically.

"Throw them. Into the door," Tanic said.

I hurled one at the door. It struck haft first and bounced back towards us. Ravenblood dove for cover. I was too surprised to do anything but watch as it landed at my feet.

Tanic guffawed.

"Maybe you should just go to the pub. You could never learn how to throw a dart."

I glared at him. This country bumpkin wasn't going to show me up on such a simple thing as sticking a piece of metal into a door. I took a long draught of the ale from my bota and started hurling the things at the door in earnest. Every time I missed, they bounced off the door and landed handily at my feet.

After a couple of hours of practice, I was, well, not exactly good, but at least competent at sticking them in the door.

NINJA SKILLS ARE FAR EASIER TO ACQUIRE WITH PRACTICE THAN FIGHTER SKILLS FOR THE SIMPLE REASON THAT THEY DON'T REQUIRE ACTUAL COMBAT. THE INITIAL BATTLES WITH THE GLOPS COMING OUT OF THE HALL WILL HELP TO RAISE NINJA SKILLS, BUT STATIC PRACTICE IS EQUALLY IMPORTANT. A DOOR OR TREE IS GOOD FOR PRACTICE. JUST STAND IN FRONT OF IT AND THROW DARTS. THEY WILL SIMPLY BOUNCE OFF AND LAND RIGHT IN FRONT OF YOU, MAKING THEM EASY TO RETRIEVE (UNLIKE IN ACTUAL COMBAT, WHERE THEY WILL OFTEN STICK IN THE MONSTER). NINJA SKILLS SHOULD COME QUICKLY. WHEN THE PARTY LEADER HAS GAINED A QUICK LEVEL OR TWO IN THIS MANNER, SWITCH LEADERS UNTIL EVERYONE HAS HAD A CHANCE TO DEVELOP IN THIS IMPORTANT AREA.

SLASH ATTACKS WITH DAGGERS IN MELEE WILL ALSO RAISE NINJA SKILL LEVELS CONSIDERABLY. ALTHOUGH THEY ARE NOT AS DAMAGING AS LARGER WEAPONS, THE HIGH SPEED WITH WHICH THEY CAN BE WIELDED MAKES UP FOR THEIR DEFICIENCY.

THROWING IS PERFORMED BY DROPPING AN OBJECT IN THE TOP HALF OF THE SCREEN. SIMPLY MOVE THE OBJECT YOU WISH TO THROW TO THE UPPER HALF OF THE SCREEN AND CLICK TO DROP IT.

And the strange part of it was that I really was rather enjoying the whole thing.

I turned around to brag to Tanic about my wonderous new skill, but I found he and the now awake Zilch were sitting on the ground with potion bottles in front of them, listening to Ravenblood lecture.

"And when you are creating the essence, be sure to catch it all in the potion bottle," he was saying.

Basic spell-casting technique for a potion. I already had a passing familiarity with the strange clerical habit of making potions, but I sat and practiced with them anyway, just to brush up. As with ale, you never can have too many healing potions.

USE THE FOUR POTION BOTTLES YOU WILL fIND AROUND THE VILLAGE TO PRACTICE YOUR CLERICAL SKILLS. GET RID OF WHATEVER IS IN THE BOTTLES WHEN YOU fIND THEM AND GIVE ONE OF THE EMPTIES TO EACH OF THE PARTY MEMBERS. PUT A STAFF IN THE OTHER HAND OF THE HEROES WHO OBVIOUSLY NEED THE EXTRA MANA. THEN CHOOSE ANY CHAMPION AND HAVE THE CHAMPION WEAR THE TECH HELM TO GAIN EXTRA WISDOM. BEGIN CASTING WITH LO VI AND, IF SUCCESSFUL, DRINK THE POTION AND TRY UM VI, AND SO ON. AFTER THE fIRST FAILURE, CONCENTRATE ON THAT LEVEL OF HEALING POTION UNTIL A NEW SKILL LEVEL IS ATTAINED. SLEEP AS NEEDED TO REGAIN LOST MANA.

THE SAME SORT OF PRACTICE IS RECOMMENDED WITH WIZARD SPELLS, BUT THE ONE TO CONCENTRATE ON IS FIREBALL, SINCE IT IS THE MOST READILY USED WIZARD SPELL.

After practice, I proceeded to have a nightcap at the pub, where Ravenblood joined me.

"We aren't going to be able to get out of this are we?"

I thought about it a second.

"No, I don't think so. But we can at least get another day's reprieve. I'll teach the dullards to use a Fireball. That should keep them amused."

"Trying to teach those two magick," he snorted. "At least we have plenty of job security."

I raised my glass to that.

We spent all the next day working on Fireballs. The Fireballs seemed to make most of the shopkeepers rather nervous, but when they tried to complain I would make ominous threatening gestures at their shops, and they would go back in and prepare buckets of water to put out the small fires being started by the less mentally adept pupils.

But I found there was only so much they could learn. No matter how hard I tried to drill the concepts into them, they just weren't progressing any more by the end of the day. Unfortunately, the time was at hand to actually go out and fight something.

Out in the wilds.

Away from pubs.

I found the thought more than a little disturbing.

After a bit, you will find that level progression is no longer occurring through practice. At this point, it is time to go out and adventure. After slaying a few monsters and getting some on-the-job training with your new skills, you will find that practice will again bring about level advancement. Continue to practice throughout your adventures; it will greatly increase your proficiency in combat.

Magick and Stuff

Ah, yes, those were the days. I will tell you the rest of tale before we are done here tonight, but now it is more important to make sure you are properly schooled in the ways of magick.

I am positively parched. Explaining all this is thirsty work. Barkeep! Another round here.

Now, where was I? Ah, yes, magick. Quite frankly I am simply astounded at how lax the mage's guild is here. Yea, they take your dues, make you learn the stupid secret handshake and signs, but they don't teach you the spells.

But never fear. I will tell you everything you need to know about the ways of mana and magic. Every spell, every magickal item. And once we are done, you will be able to use authority when dealing with all the magickal matters you might run across. Who knows, after you settle down from adventuring you might make some extra money doing small shows and birthday parties.

Spells

Learning your spells is the most important thing you can do to prepare for the journey. Given, there are all manner of magickal aids out there, but money is hard to come by, and thieves and other obstacles can separate you from your items. A good spell, however, never leaves you and cannot be stolen.

Priest Spells

Priest spells are mainly of the protection and healing variety. While not in some ways as handy during adventuring as the incantations for the wizards, these spells, when properly used, are still a great boon to your party.

Priest Spells

YA Stamina Potion

The stamina potion, surprisingly, raises the stamina of the imbiber. This is important for helping out after an extremely exhausting retreat or for providing sustenance should the party run out of food.

YA IR Party Shield

This spell protects from attacks by normal weapons. If you are surrounded and your spell-casters are lightly armored, this spell can be the difference between life and death for the wizards and priests.

YA IR DAIN Shield Potion

Shield potions give defense against normal weapons for one who drinks it.

YA BRO DAIN Wisdom Potion

A potion that increases the wisdom, this will help considerably with the casting of spells.

YA BRO NETA Vitality Potion

A vitality booster. When the vitality is improved, it will assist with healing and recovery of stamina.

VI Health

This potion gives health to a damaged hero. It is the only way to heal a champion's wounds. This spell is used a great deal, so focus your practice on it.

VI BRO Cure Poison

A quick cure-poison potion can save a hero from lingering death by poison. Use one of these as quickly as possible on a poisoned character.

OH EW KU Aura of Strength

This aura increases the strength of all members of the party.

OH EW ROS Aura of Dexterity

This aura increases the dexterity of all party members. Combined with the Aura of Strength, it will make the party a fearsome fighting unit, indeed.

OH EW NETA Aura of Vitality

This spell produces an aura around the party that increases the vitality of all of your heroes.

OH BRO ROS Dexterity Potion

This potion increases the dexterity of a hero who quaffs it, making the hero more difficult for the monsters to strike. It will also improve the hero's accuracy in his or her attacks.

FUL BRO KU Strength Potion

This potion will increase the strength attribute, allowing a champion to wield heavier weapons and do more damage with whatever weapon is used.

FUL BRO NETA Fireshield

This spell envelops each party member in a glowing shield that is resistant to fire. The higher the level of the spell, the stronger the shield becomes.

DES IR SAR Darkness

When these runes are invoked, a spherical shell of darkness will surround the party. This often allows the party to escape from a particularly vicious monster.

ZO EW ROS Porter Minion

The Porter Minion summoned with this incantation can take some of the load off the party. When it is summoned, this spirit will pick up all objects in the square. Then it will follow two steps behind the party wherever they may lead.

ZO EW NETA Guard Minion

The Guard Minion, as we will discuss in a few moments, is probably the single most important spell in the world. This spell creates a Guard Minion who will attack any hostile creatures that come near it. At higher levels, this creature is quite a force to be dealt with.

ZO BRO RA Mana Potion

This spell creates a potion that gives mana back to the caster. The amount of mana regained is less than half of that required to create the potion. However, this spell is good to use at the end of a day to create a "mana battery" for later use during harder times.

ZO BRO ROS Reflector Spell

Working this incantation produces a short-lived shield that will reflect all spells back at their caster. Having a problem getting that pesky numen staff? This is just the spell for that kind of work. If we had used this one when fighting Dragoth during our glorious and heroic, er, thrashing, well, things might have turned out a bit differently.

Wizard Spells

YA EW Magick Marker

This spell produces a magick stone which can be used to mark locations. The magickal maps will show the locations of magick markers when the "show magick" option is activated.

OH VEN Poison Cloud

This enchantment produces a cloud of noxious smoke that will cause disarray in most groups of monsters, forcing them to cast about for a way to escape the cloud or retreat entirely. While there are many juvenile wisecracks leveled at wizards who use this spell quickly, it can provide a party with a quick respite during combat.

OH EW SAR Invisibility

Invisibility causes the party to fade from normal vision. While this spell tends to lend itself to all sorts of great sneaky things done in combat, don't forget that some monsters rely on smell or infrared light to track their prey and will not be fooled.

OH KATH KU Push

This spell simply pushes a creature or object one square back from the party. It can push more weight the higher level at which the spell is cast.

OH KATH ROS Pull

This spell has the opposite effect of Push: It moves a creature or object one square away from the party to you. However, if there isn't an open square between the party and creature, this spell will fail.

OH KATH RA Lightning

This is one of those spells that gives us sorcerers a great reputation. A bolt of lighting flies from the fingertips of the caster and keeps going until it evaporates or hits something and explodes.

OH IR ROS Accelerate Party

This spell makes the movement of the party temporarily speed up. This allows a party to move through a dungeon at a very high speed or get extra hits on an offending group of monsters.

OH IR RA Strong Light

A ball of light that wafts along with the party is produced by this spell. It is both brighter and longer lasting than the Firelight spell.

FUL Firelight

This spell produces a dim ball of light that follows the party like a hungry puppy. This spell takes about half as much mana to cast as strong light, which is the only reason it stays on the books at all.

FUL IR Fireball

Fireball is the bread and butter of the traveling sorcerer. A great ball of fire flies from the outstretched hand of the caster and travels until it dissipates or hits something and explodes in a great hail of heat and pain. While some creatures are immune to the effects of fire, there are many more who will find a quick death at the hands of this spell.

DES VEN Poison Foe

This spell is the big brother of Poison Cloud. Instead of creating a cloud, it simply poisons the targeted creature directly. In most instances, this will result in the immediate death of the unfortunate target. However, if the creature remains standing, it will be able to continue attacking the party.

DES EW Harm Non-Material

Although there isn't too much call for this spell, when you need it, you really need it. This spell and the vorpal sword are the only two things that can harm some creatures. So keeping this spell ready is always a good idea.

ZO Open Door

I personally think it is below wizards to have to deal with anything but magickal portals, but this spell, when cast, will open or close all unlocked doors that have buttons, and it will do so from a distance. The much more important function of this spell is that it will close the small void portals that many evil minions of Dragoth use to enter your dimension.

ZO EW KU Attack Minion

Attack Minions are wonderful little creatures that can be summoned to cast lightning bolts at all enemy creatures until they are dead or until the minion is destroyed. Much like the Guard Minion, the attack minion becomes a really formidable fighter when cast at higher levels.

Wizard Spells

These are the bread and butter of your combat spell-casting. Let's just drop all the false modesty, shall we! Wizards are the ultimate adventurers. Without us, the rest of you would be nothing! We are nearly deities! YOU SHOULD BOW DOWN BEFORE US!

Uh, pardon me. I'm back under control. You can let go of me now.

I might have gotten a bit presumptuous. However, it is true that, when in combat, a few well-placed wizard spells will often mean the difference between success and failure.

But before you can cast them, you need to know them.

Magick Items

While spells are the bread and butter of the adventuring party, magick items have their place. Many items will allow the user to cast spells either off of their mana or off of the item's mana, a particularly useful ability for those times when mana might be running a bit low but the monsters aren't. However, conserving an item's mana as much as possible is always a good choice, since very few items can be recharged.

What follows is a list of those items with magickal properties, broken down into armor, weapons, and general items. Note that while many items of armor provide their protection by being magickal in nature, only those items that have a spell effect or that give unnatural bonuses to their wearer are listed here.

Armor

The following is a list of the Magickal Armors to be found on your travels.

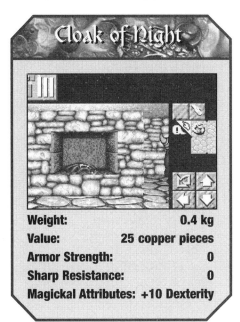

Cloak of Night

Weight:	0.4 kg
Value:	25 copper pieces
Armor Strength:	0
Sharp Resistance:	0
Magickal Attributes:	+10 Dexterity

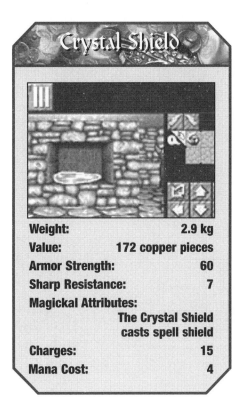

Crystal Shield

Weight:	2.9 kg
Value:	172 copper pieces
Armor Strength:	60
Sharp Resistance:	7
Magickal Attributes:	The Crystal Shield casts spell shield
Charges:	15
Mana Cost:	4

Fire Helmet

Weight:	2.1 kg
Value:	400 copper pieces
Armor Strength:	54
Sharp Resistance:	6
Magickal Attributes:	+10 Anti-fire

Fire Shield

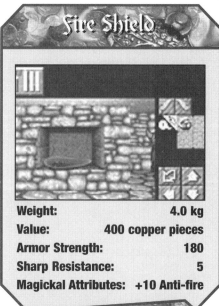

Weight:	4.0 kg
Value:	400 copper pieces
Armor Strength:	180
Sharp Resistance:	5
Magickal Attributes:	+10 Anti-fire

Fire Poleyn

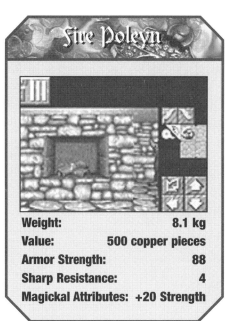

Weight:	8.1 kg
Value:	500 copper pieces
Armor Strength:	88
Sharp Resistance:	4
Magickal Attributes:	+20 Strength

Mithral Hosen

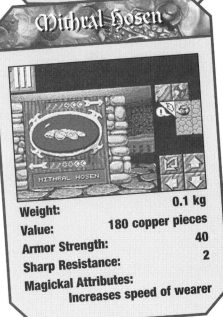

Weight:	0.1 kg
Value:	180 copper pieces
Armor Strength:	40
Sharp Resistance:	2
Magickal Attributes:	Increases speed of wearer

NOTES:

Mithral Hosen will increase the speed of whoever wears them, but they will still be limited by the overall party speed. Since only two of these items are known to be at large in the world, their value might seem questionable. However, there is one good use for them. If characters are killed and only one or two champions are left to transport their remains to the resurrection altar, then put on the hose. The extra speed will help avoid monsters and considerably speed up the return journey.

RA SAR Helm

Weight:	1.7 kg
Value:	300 copper pieces
Armor Strength:	62
Sharp Resistance:	5
Magickal Attributes:	+15 Dexterity

RA SAR Shield

Weight:	unknown
Value:	unknown
Armor Strength:	0
Sharp Resistance:	0
Magickal Attributes:	+10 Dexterity

RA SAR Plate

Weight:	7.5 kg
Value:	700 copper pieces
Armor Strength:	125
Sharp Resistance:	6
Magickal Attributes:	+20 Mana Weak Invisibility Spell

Techelm

Weight:	3.5 kg
Value:	590 copper pieces
Armor Strength:	76
Sharp Resistance:	4
Magickal Attributes:	+15 Wisdom

Tech Shield

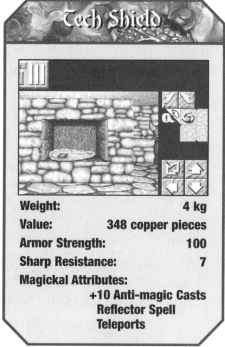

Weight:	4 kg
Value:	348 copper pieces
Armor Strength:	100
Sharp Resistance:	7
Magickal Attributes:	
	+10 Anti-magic Casts
	Reflector Spell
	Teleports

Tech Plate

Weight:	14.1 kg
Value:	1250 copper pieces
Armor Strength:	160
Sharp Resistance:	4
Magickal Attributes:	+30 Anti-magic

NOTES:

This shield is a great item, as it not only gives the ability to teleport and cast the Reflector Spell, but it also doesn't require any mana and has no charges.

Weapons

Magickal Weapons have one heck of a reputation. Where would any great hero be without his famous magickal blade of cleaving! You ever hear great epics sung in barrooms about "Maldrik, with the great magical socks, the Darnless Pair?" No, you don't. So here is your guide to all the great weapons of the realm, which you are going to need to acquire if you ever expect them to sing about you.

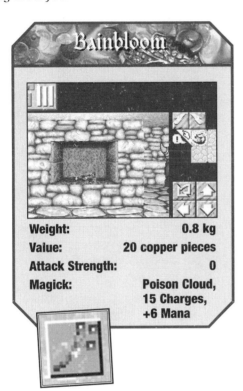

Bainbloom

Weight:	0.8 kg
Value:	20 copper pieces
Attack Strength:	0
Magick:	Poison Cloud, 15 Charges, +6 Mana

NOTES:

This item will not heal injuries, but will repair general problems. The attack ability and mana addition make it a fine staff.

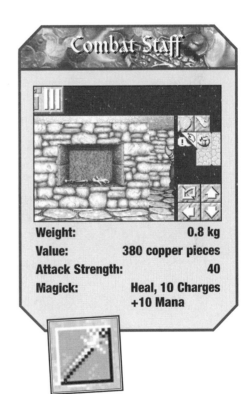

Combat Staff

Weight:	0.8 kg
Value:	380 copper pieces
Attack Strength:	40
Magick:	Heal, 10 Charges +10 Mana

Emerald Orb

Weight:	2.9 kg
Value:	260 copper pieces
Armor Strength:	15
Magickal:	Calm, Heal and Poison Foe, 15 Charges, +30 Mana

Excsymyr

Weight:	3.3 kg
Value:	350 copper pieces
Attack Strength:	50
Magick:	+10 Mana

Eye of Time

Weight:	0.1 kg
Value:	2200 copper pieces
Attack Strength:	0
Magick:	Freeze all creatures attacking once or instead cast. Accelerate on the party three times.

Fury

Weight:	4.7 kg
Value:	1100 copper pieces
Attack Strength:	55

Magick: Medium Fireball, 15 Charges. Also provides light, but this slowly sucks off stored mana.

Kalan Gauntlet

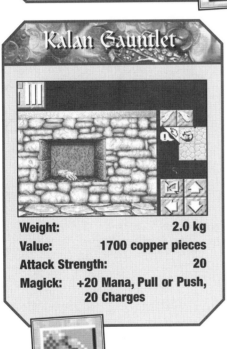

Weight:	2.0 kg
Value:	1700 copper pieces
Attack Strength:	20

Magick: +20 Mana, Pull or Push, 20 Charges

Staff of META

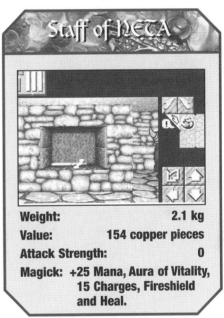

Weight:	2.1 kg
Value:	154 copper pieces
Attack Strength:	0

Magick: +25 Mana, Aura of Vitality, 15 Charges, Fireshield and Heal.

NOTES:

This is a valuable staff. First it allows healing to take place without the annoying flask procedure required for the spell potion. The mana and fireshield are added benefits.

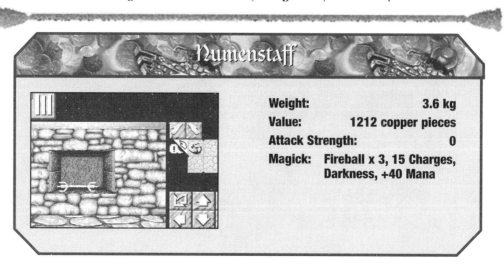

Numenstaff

Weight:	3.6 kg
Value:	1212 copper pieces
Attack Strength:	0
Magick:	Fireball x 3, 15 Charges, Darkness, +40 Mana

Notes:

This item can be fully recharged by being placed in the cauldron near where it is found. While the fireballs that it casts aren't of the most powerful variety, this really doesn't matter because there are plenty of them.

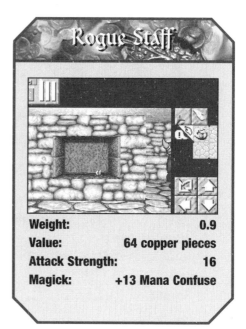

Rogue Staff

Weight:	0.9
Value:	64 copper pieces
Attack Strength:	16
Magick:	+13 Mana Confuse

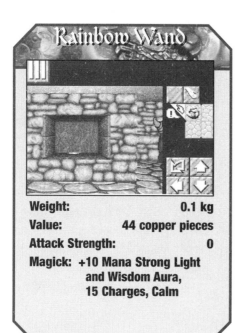

Rainbow Wand

Weight:	0.1 kg
Value:	44 copper pieces
Attack Strength:	0
Magick:	+10 Mana Strong Light and Wisdom Aura, 15 Charges, Calm

Scarab

Weight:	0.8 kg
Value:	180 copper pieces
Attack Strength:	0
Magick:	Party Shield, 1 Charge

Serpent Staff

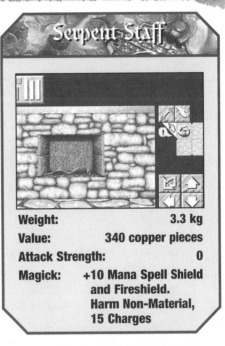

Weight:	3.3 kg
Value:	340 copper pieces
Attack Strength:	0
Magick:	+10 Mana Spell Shield and Fireshield. Harm Non-Material, 15 Charges

Spiral Staff

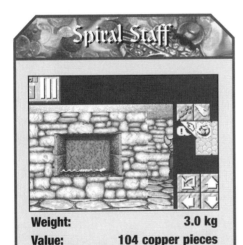

Weight:	3.0 kg
Value:	104 copper pieces
Attack Strength:	9
Magick:	+15 Mana, Aura of Dexterity and Lightning, 10 Charges

Staff

Weight:	2.6 kg
Value:	7 copper pieces
Attack Strength:	12
Magick:	+5 Mana. Firelight, Open Door, 3 Charges

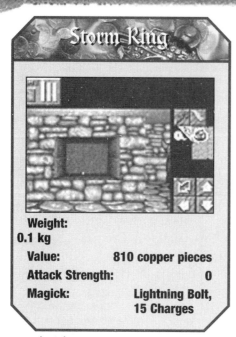

Storm Ring

Weight:	
0.1 kg	
Value:	810 copper pieces
Attack Strength:	0
Magick:	Lightning Bolt, 15 Charges

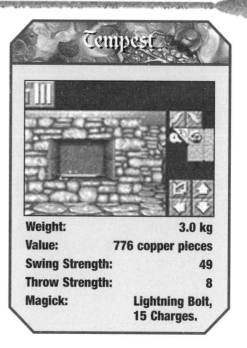

Tempest

Weight:	3.0 kg
Value:	776 copper pieces
Swing Strength:	49
Throw Strength:	8
Magick:	Lightning Bolt, 15 Charges.

General Objects

Sometimes, even in the most common piece of jewelry or daily object, some magickal property might lurk.

For instance, pick a card, any card.

Okay, now look at it and put it back in the deck.

This one is your card, isn't it!

See, there are magickal items everywhere. I like to call this the Deck of the Stupid Shill. Should be available at all fine magickal purveyors throughout the land by Fall season at the latest.

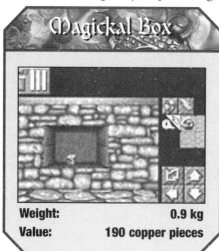

Magickal Box

Weight:	0.9 kg
Value:	190 copper pieces

NOTES:

This box can cast Freeze or Haste and has one charge.

Illumulet

Weight: 0.2 kg
Value: 89 copper pieces

NOTES:

Produces a weak light.

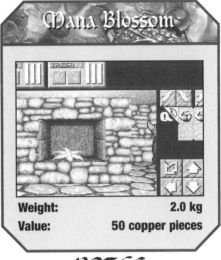

Mana Blossom

Weight: 2.0 kg
Value: 50 copper pieces

NOTES:

Mana blossoms provide +15 Mana, but only to the current mana of the hero. They do not increase the total mana the hero may attain. Mana blossoms also have a small nutritional value.

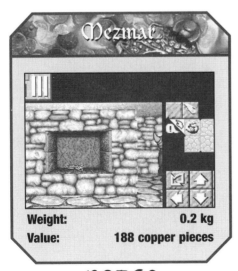

Mezmar

Weight: 0.2 kg
Value: 188 copper pieces

NOTES:

+5 Dexterity.

Moon-Stone

Weight: 0.2 kg
Value: 130 copper pieces

NOTES:

+3 Mana

Meteor Metal

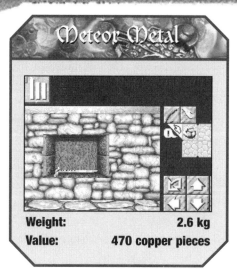

Weight:	2.6 kg
Value:	470 copper pieces

NOTES:

This is the blank for a Blue Steele sword, which may be created by putting the Meteor Metal in the Numen cauldron.

Jewel of Symal

Weight:	0.2 kg
Value:	54 copper pieces

NOTES:

+6 Anti-fire.

Fairy Cushion

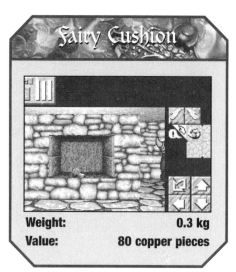

Weight:	0.3 kg
Value:	80 copper pieces

NOTES:

These toadstools temporarily reduce vitality 20 to 30 points and raise strength by 20.

Suzerain

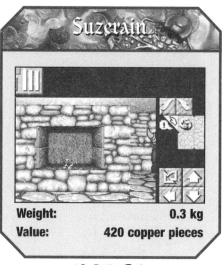

Weight:	0.3 kg
Value:	420 copper pieces

NOTES:

+10 Mana.

Spirit Cap

Weight:	0.3 kg
Value:	120 copper pieces

NOTES:

-20 Vitality.

Magick Map

Weight:	0.3 kg
Value:	100+ copper pieces

NOTES:

These maps, explained elsewhere in much more detail, help the party to determine what is in their immediate environment and can even summon minions to do the bidding of the party.

Advanced Use of Magick

There is very little to really remember about the proper use of magick. Now that you know the available spells and magickal items, most things are pretty self-explanatory. I guess you probably think you are ready to just leap up and go out fighting, right!

Wrong! See there, this is why wizards are superior to the rest of you, we think things out more thoroughly.

Let go of my robes.

Choke, gasp.

Okay, I take it back.

Ahem. If you are going to be that way about it then, I guess I will just get right to the point. All the spells are well and good, but in real life ninety percent of the spells you are going to be casting are Fireball, Accelerate, Health Potion and Guard Minion.

Fireballs are one of the most consistent monster slayers in the grimore. Having one of these ready at every encounter just makes good sense. Very few monsters are able to take a good fireball, much less a few fireballs.

Accelerate gives your fighters the jump-start they need to really hammer on any foes.

The Health Potion is pretty obvious. No matter how swift you are with the fireballs and Accelerate, you are going to take some damage.

Now at this point you are saying to yourself, I am buying this guy drinks to listen to this obvious stuff! Well, open your ears as I earn my tab.

Give me some ground to stand on, a bit of time and the runes to cast Guard Minion and I can rule the world. As a matter of a fact, I don't cast Guard Minion all that much simply because I feel it is inhumane to do that to the monsters. If you get most of your party up to the point where you can cast this spell moderately well, you will become invincible.

Guard Minion blocks your enemies, pelts them with lightning bolts from two spaces away and absorbs heinous amounts of damage.

Now, if you were an honorable chap, you would only use one or two of these creatures now and then to help you out of tight spots. But are we going to do that? With the universe on the line here! Heck no! Drop Guard Minions like you are spreading grass seed. Send as many of them as you can produce into every fight that looks like it might cause you to break a nail!

The minions will surround your foes and catch them in a utterly destroying crossfire while getting underfoot to the point of creating impenetrable barriers.

The lower levels of this spell are bad enough, but when you get to the MON version, it is basically the end of the world. Trust me on this. When you can cast at that level, you aren't far from retirement on the beach, with Dragoth as your houseboy.

Bad Guys

The whole adventuring thing, actually, might not be so bleak if it was just a matter of marching up to the baddie, taking your shot and seeing who came out on top. But, unfortunately, you not only have to slog though a plethora of traps, tricks, and other nasty bits, but you must contend with the creatures.

Some creatures spit fire, some creatures are wet and slimy, and they never seem to be in the proper order to make life easy. I mean, you deal with a slime creature, then you wouldn't mind dealing with a fire creature, now would you? Warm you up a bit.

Unfortunately, they come in every order imaginable, and you just have to hack and cast your way though them. Here in my notes I have a list of every creature we came across in our quest and all the data I was able to magickally glean about them. If you would care to leaf through it, I will make comments where appropriate.

Archer Guard

Habitat: Castle

Hit Points: 420

Weight: 110

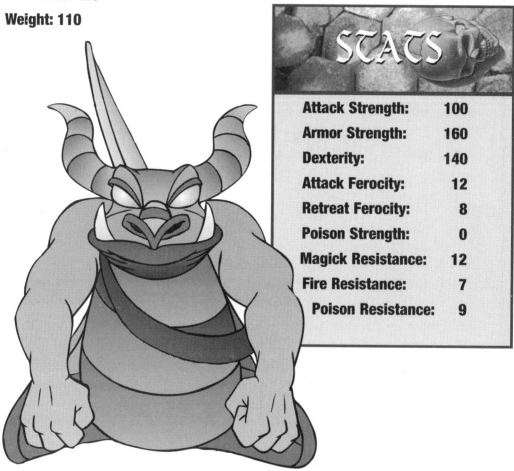

STATS

Attack Strength:	100
Armor Strength:	160
Dexterity:	140
Attack Ferocity:	12
Retreat Ferocity:	8
Poison Strength:	0
Magick Resistance:	12
Fire Resistance:	7
Poison Resistance:	9

These nasty creatures are the final minions between you and Dragoth, and they are just the kind of foe to ruin your entire week. Not only do they stay away from fighters and dodge anything fired at them, they also will use your own slayer arrows, firing them back at you. These beasties are notoriously hard to kill.

Attack Minion

Habitat: All Areas

Hit Points: 100-150

Weight: 10

STATS

Attack Strength:	8-50
Armor Strength:	75
Dexterity:	180
Attack Ferocity:	9-14
Retreat Ferocity:	14-15
Poison Strength:	0
Magick Resistance:	15
Fire Resistance:	7-13
Poison Resistance:	12

Attack Minions are summoned by spell and will attack all enemies in range and then dissipate. The only thing to remember about these creatures is to let them do their job if they are on your side. Stray into their line of fire and you will be hit by their bolts.

On the other hand, when they are on the other team, Attack Minions are a real problem. They are fast and avoid missile attacks quite well. Point-blank fireballs are one way of dealing with these creatures. Another, fairly obvious, way to handle them is to set your own minions on them.

Axeman

Habitat: Thicket

Hit Points: 175

Weight: 70

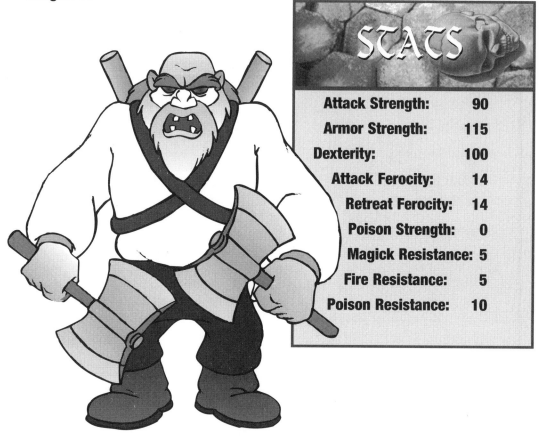

STATS

Attack Strength:	90
Armor Strength:	115
Dexterity:	100
Attack Ferocity:	14
Retreat Ferocity:	14
Poison Strength:	0
Magick Resistance:	5
Fire Resistance:	5
Poison Resistance:	10

First seen in the distance, these creatures will throw axes at you and then close to attack in melee. Some will also steal from you. Beware, it isn't often you see just a few Axemen, they like large groups. Guard Minions and close-range fireballs are the best ways of dispatching Axemen. Close-range fighting is not recommended, as Axemen do a great deal of damage with their multiple melee attacks.

Bad Merchant

Habitat: Village

Hit Points: 1,000

Weight: 110

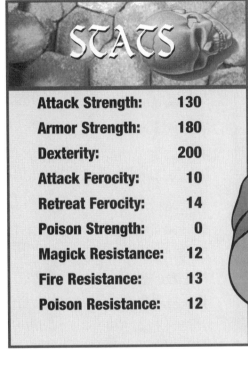

STATS

Attack Strength:	130
Armor Strength:	180
Dexterity:	200
Attack Ferocity:	10
Retreat Ferocity:	14
Poison Strength:	0
Magick Resistance:	12
Fire Resistance:	13
Poison Resistance:	12

These merchants are the shady operators of the merchant race. They buy and sell most anything and have a unique group of items of questionable lineage to sell and are more than willing to buy smost anything. Obviously, attacking one is just as foolhardy as trying to attack one of their more upright kin.

Bat

Habitat: Castle, Roof, Cavern

Hit Points: 30

Weight: 10

Outside of caves, bats will rarely attack adventurers, but if cornered in caves they will violently defend their homes. Dead Bats are edible for those with strong stomachs and are worth 2 silver coins at a pub.

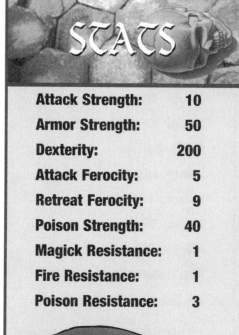

STATS

Attack Strength:	10
Armor Strength:	50
Dexterity:	200
Attack Ferocity:	5
Retreat Ferocity:	9
Poison Strength:	40
Magick Resistance:	1
Fire Resistance:	1
Poison Resistance:	3

Fetch/Carry Minion

Habitat: All Areas

Hit Points: 100-150

Weight: 10

STATS

Attack Strength:	8-50
Armor Strength:	75
Dexterity:	180
Attack Ferocity:	9-14
Retreat Ferocity:	14-15
Poison Strength:	0
Magick Resistance:	15
Fire Resistance:	7-13
Poison Resistance:	12

Fetch and Carry Minions are products of one of the Magick Maps and were covered earlier in my tale.

Dragoth

Habitat: Void

Hit Points: 1,500

Weight: 254

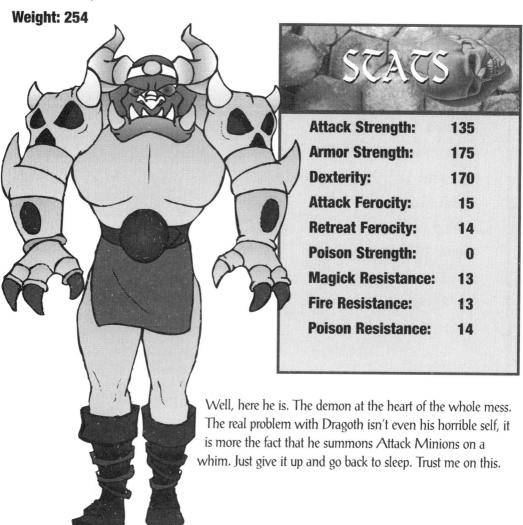

STATS

Attack Strength:	135
Armor Strength:	175
Dexterity:	170
Attack Ferocity:	15
Retreat Ferocity:	14
Poison Strength:	0
Magick Resistance:	13
Fire Resistance:	13
Poison Resistance:	14

Well, here he is. The demon at the heart of the whole mess. The real problem with Dragoth isn't even his horrible self, it is more the fact that he summons Attack Minions on a whim. Just give it up and go back to sleep. Trust me on this.

Dru-Tan

Habitat: Cavern

Hit Points: 600

Weight: 254

STATS

Attack Strength:	160
Armor Strength:	220
Dexterity:	120
Attack Ferocity:	11
Retreat Ferocity:	12
Poison Strength:	0
Magick Resistance:	8
Fire Resistance:	8
Poison Resistance:	11

Dru-Tan isn't all that bright, and even if he should defeat you, there is a good chance he will shove you into a pit instead of killing you. You never can tell. Rather reminds me of Zilch . . .

Flame Orb

Habitat: Cavern

Hit Points: 80

Weight: 20

Flame Orbs are magical creatures that will blow themselves up in the party's midst, given half a chance. The very rapid use of a DES EW spell or a Vorpal Blade will give you a respite from these living bombs.

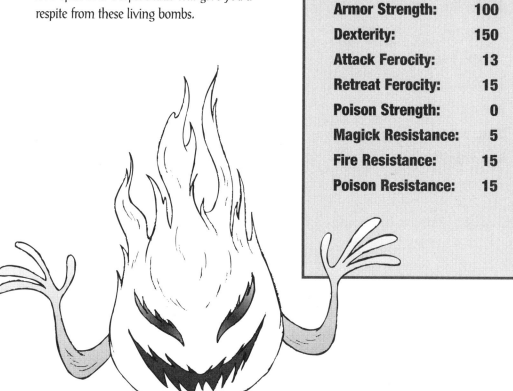

STATS

Attack Strength:	100
Armor Strength:	100
Dexterity:	150
Attack Ferocity:	13
Retreat Ferocity:	15
Poison Strength:	0
Magick Resistance:	5
Fire Resistance:	15
Poison Resistance:	15

Imp

Habitat: Castle

Hit Points: 135

Weight: 70

Imps are basically a magickally augmented version of a thief. They are so quick that they can steal items right out of an adventurer's hands.

STATS

Attack Strength:	20
Armor Strength:	50
Dexterity:	240
Attack Ferocity:	15
Retreat Ferocity:	13
Poison Strength:	0
Magick Resistance:	15
Fire Resistance:	4
Poison Resistance:	4

Glop

Habitat: Thicket

Hit Points: 36

Weight: 65

Glops are slow and easy to kill. The only thing notable about the glop is its habit of swallowing items in its travels, so always be sure to inspect a glop carcass for possible treasure.

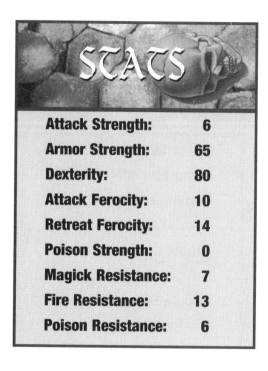

STATS	
Attack Strength:	6
Armor Strength:	65
Dexterity:	80
Attack Ferocity:	10
Retreat Ferocity:	14
Poison Strength:	0
Magick Resistance:	7
Fire Resistance:	13
Poison Resistance:	6

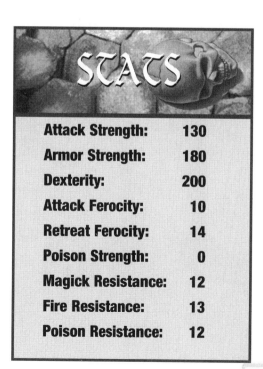

STATS	
Attack Strength:	130
Armor Strength:	180
Dexterity:	200
Attack Ferocity:	10
Retreat Ferocity:	14
Poison Strength:	0
Magick Resistance:	12
Fire Resistance:	13
Poison Resistance:	12

Magick Merchant

Habitat: Cloud Clan Area

Hit Points: 1,000

Weight: 110

Hard to find, the Magick Merchants are just what their name implies: They traffic in the hard-to-find Magickal items.

Merchant

Habitat: Sun Clan Village

Hit Points: 1,000

Weight: 110

The Merchants are traders who supply all the basic needs of an adventuring party, for a price. Attacking them, for a variety of reasons, is instant suicide.

STATS	
Attack Strength:	130
Armor Strength:	180
Dexterity:	200
Attack Ferocity:	10
Retreat Ferocity:	14
Poison Strength:	0
Magick Resistance:	12
Fire Resistance:	13
Poison Resistance:	12

Magick Guard

Habitat: Village

Hit Points: 1,000

Weight: 110

This is the main reason that attacking a merchant is suicide. These creatures will instantly and ferociously attack anyone who tries to harm one of their kindred, the Merchants.

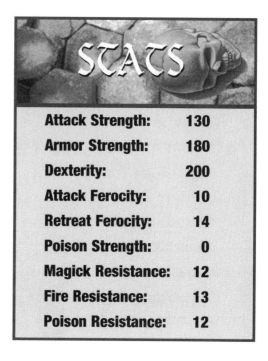

STATS

Attack Strength:	130
Armor Strength:	180
Dexterity:	200
Attack Ferocity:	10
Retreat Ferocity:	14
Poison Strength:	0
Magick Resistance:	12
Fire Resistance:	13
Poison Resistance:	12

Mummy

Habitat: Tomb

Hit Points: 50

Weight: 50

STATS

Attack Strength:	35
Armor Strength:	70
Dexterity:	60
Attack Ferocity:	12
Retreat Ferocity:	14
Poison Strength:	0
Magick Resistance:	15
Fire Resistance:	3
Poison Resistance:	15

Bandages with an attitude, Mummys are easy pickings for anything but the weakest parties.

Rocky

Habitat: Cavern

Hit Points: 150

Weight: 70

Rockies are annoying little critters that will throw rocks at most anything in their vicinity. However, the Rockies are instrumental in getting to Dragoth, as I will explain later. So don't just kill them without thinking through the repercussions of your actions.

STATS

Attack Strength:	40
Armor Strength:	80
Dexterity:	80
Attack Ferocity:	10
Retreat Ferocity:	8
Poison Strength:	0
Magic Resistance:	12
Fire Resistance:	12
Poison Resistance:	9

Scout Minion

Habitat: All Areas

Hit Points: 100-150

Weight: 10

These minions are just what their name implies. They scout out the territory ahead of the party to describe what unseen dangers might lie in the shadows. Scout Minions are a powerful addition to a party's intelligence gathering ability.

STATS

Attack Strength:	8-50
Armor Strength:	75
Dexterity:	180
Attack Ferocity:	9-14
Retreat Ferocity:	14-15
Poison Strength:	0
Magick Resistance:	15
Fire Resistance:	7-13
Poison Resistance:	12

Skeleton

Habitat: Cavern

Hit Points: 175

Weight: 55

Skeletons are best fought with very strong magic, an axe, or a mace.

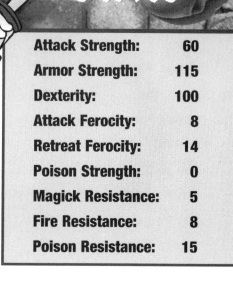

STATS

Attack Strength:	60
Armor Strength:	115
Dexterity:	100
Attack Ferocity:	8
Retreat Ferocity:	14
Poison Strength:	0
Magick Resistance:	5
Fire Resistance:	8
Poison Resistance:	15

Spectre

Habitat: Graveyard

Hit Points: 150

Weight: 255

STATS

Attack Strength:	2
Armor Strength:	100
Dexterity:	150
Attack Ferocity:	15
Retreat Ferocity:	12
Poison Strength:	0
Magick Resistance:	6
Fire Resistance:	15
Poison Resistance:	15

Spectres are the remains of cursed souls. Because they are magickal creatures, most forms of damage have very little effect on them. Use Vorpal Blade or the DES EW spell to break the magick and send them to the nether reaches where they belong.

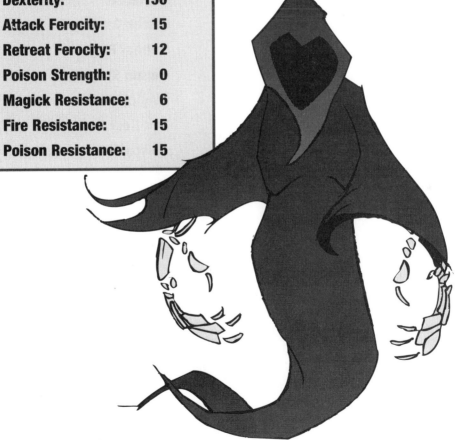

Thief

Habitat: Thicket

Hit Points: 175

Weight: 45

Often found with wolves, the Thief steals anything that isn't bolted to the floor and many things that are. Thieves duck into tunnels on a regular basis to travel to and from their lairs. However, the lucky adventurer who tracks the small creatures to their lairs will find that there is much booty secreted there. Thieves avoid missile fire quite well. The most effective method of killing them is by firing large fireballs or using large melee weapons.

STATS

Attack Strength:	35
Armor Strength:	70
Dexterity:	110
Attack Ferocity:	12
Retreat Ferocity:	7
Poison Strength:	0
Magick Resistance:	5
Fire Resistance:	5
Poison Resistance:	8

Thorn Demon

Habitat: Thicket

Hit Points: 400

Weight: 254

Thorn Demons are very dangerous to anything but an experienced party. However, they provide fine rations when finally felled.

STATS

Attack Strength:	50
Armor Strength:	85
Dexterity:	120
Attack Ferocity:	11
Retreat Ferocity:	8
Poison Strength:	0
Magick Resistance:	6
Fire Resistance:	7
Poison Resistance:	8

Tree Gorgon

Habitat: Thicket

Hit Points: 350

Weight: 255

Tree Gorgons tend to attack from out of nowhere and in great numbers. Fear and loathing precedes their eerie appearance. A quick dose of fire, however, quickly reduces tree gorgons into bonfires that lend a particularly succulent, smoky flavor to your Thorn Demon steaks.

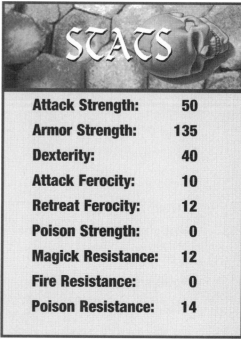

STATS

Attack Strength:	50
Armor Strength:	135
Dexterity:	40
Attack Ferocity:	10
Retreat Ferocity:	12
Poison Strength:	0
Magick Resistance:	12
Fire Resistance:	0
Poison Resistance:	14

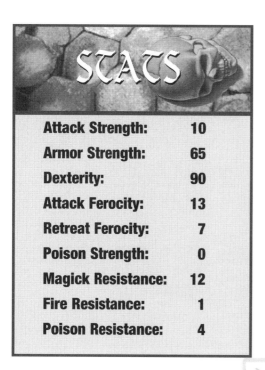

STATS

Attack Strength:	10
Armor Strength:	65
Dexterity:	90
Attack Ferocity:	13
Retreat Ferocity:	7
Poison Strength:	0
Magick Resistance:	12
Fire Resistance:	1
Poison Resistance:	4

Digger Worm

Habitat: Thicket

Hit Points: 80

Weight: 254

And while on the subject of monster cuisine, it's worth noting that Digger Worms make a fine side dish for smoked Thorn Demon steaks. However, it is rather hard to hit them, as they duck into the ground on a regular basis. Killing them requires quick reflexes. Further, they have multiple attacks that can be quite damaging to a novice party. A great deal of care should be taken with this delicacy until your champion gourmets are able to eat, as opposed to being eaten.

Dark Vexirk

Habitat: Castle

Hit Points: 150

Weight: 40

If you are willing to forgo the boon of the items used by the Vexirk they will let you pass in your mission to kill Dragoth.

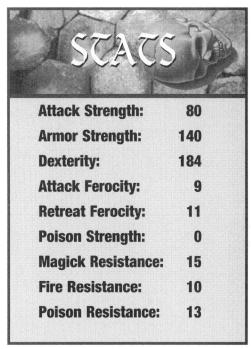

STATS	
Attack Strength:	80
Armor Strength:	140
Dexterity:	184
Attack Ferocity:	9
Retreat Ferocity:	11
Poison Strength:	0
Magick Resistance:	15
Fire Resistance:	10
Poison Resistance:	13

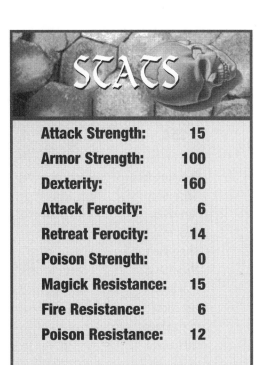

STATS	
Attack Strength:	15
Armor Strength:	100
Dexterity:	160
Attack Ferocity:	6
Retreat Ferocity:	14
Poison Strength:	0
Magick Resistance:	15
Fire Resistance:	6
Poison Resistance:	12

Vexirk King

Habitat: Castle

Hit Points: 250

Weight: 50

The Vexirk King wields the Numen staff, which is the main reason you will be unlikely to leave the Vexirk in peace. The Numen staff, detailed under magic items, is a powerful weapon which fires multiple large fireballs at a very rapid rate. The problem with this great magic item is that when you meet the Vexirk King, he has it. Fire resistance is, needless to say, very useful.

Vortex

Habitat: Thicket

Hit Points: 100

Weight: 255

Staying out of the way of the random and hard-to-damage Vortex is a good rule of thumb. However, should combat become imperative, DES EW or the Vorpal Blade should make short work of the Vortex.

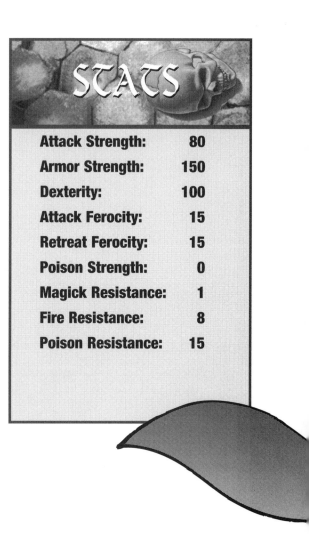

STATS

Attack Strength:	80
Armor Strength:	150
Dexterity:	100
Attack Ferocity:	15
Retreat Ferocity:	15
Poison Strength:	0
Magick Resistance:	1
Fire Resistance:	8
Poison Resistance:	15

Wolf

Habitat: Thicket

Hit Points: 150

Weight: 65

There is a simple rule for dealing with wolves: avoid them. Wolves travel in packs, meaning that you are always dealing with far too many at once. One wolf or two is easy enough to eliminate, but a constant barrage of them will wear down a party in no time.

STATS

Attack Strength:	30
Armor Strength:	90
Dexterity:	130
Attack Ferocity:	10
Retreat Ferocity:	13
Poison Strength:	0
Magick Resistance:	2
Fire Resistance:	7
Poison Resistance:	6

Worm

Habitat: Cavern

Hit Points: 250

Weight: 90

These worms aren't much of a problem for a strong party, but beware of their poison, which has felled many a hardy adventurer.

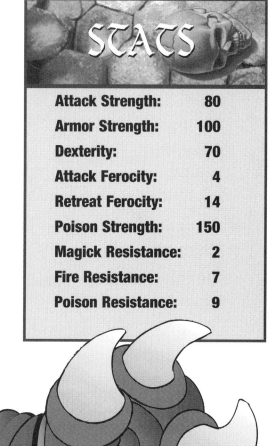

STATS

Attack Strength:	80
Armor Strength:	100
Dexterity:	70
Attack Ferocity:	4
Retreat Ferocity:	14
Poison Strength:	150
Magick Resistance:	2
Fire Resistance:	7
Poison Resistance:	9

Weapons

You know, the only problem with the world is that there aren't enough weapons in it. Oh, you meet those peace-mongers who go out and protest all the time. But when swords are outlawed, only outlaws will have swords; that's the way I feel about it.

Every once and a while, you just have to go out and lay about yourself randomly with a really big piece of steel. Only way to keep the adrenaline flowing, I say. No fun till there's a limb severed.

But if you are going to go out and really create some wanton destruction, you need the right tools. I mean, a pot-metal Saturday night special is fine for a bit of daggerplay here in town, but if you are going out in the wilds, you need some hard core steel. With this in mind, let me present you my notes on arms and armor.

Arms

The following list is a compilation of every non-magickal item in the known world that you can use to take the life of another sentient lifeform.

Arrow

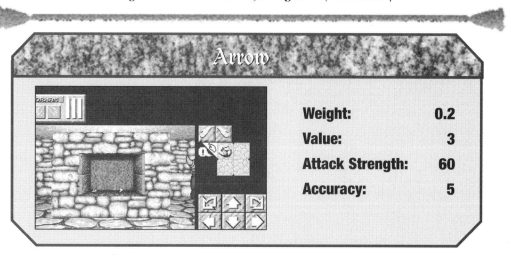

Weight:	0.2
Value:	3
Attack Strength:	60
Accuracy:	5

Ax

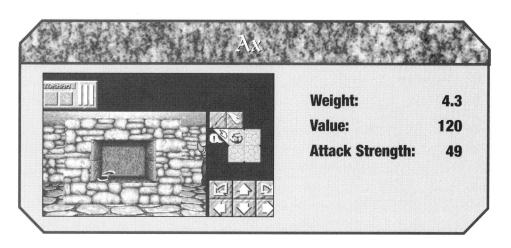

Weight:	4.3
Value:	120
Attack Strength:	49

Blue Steele

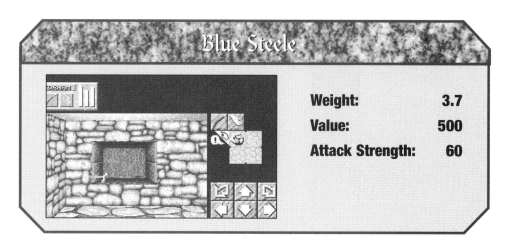

Weight:	3.7
Value:	500
Attack Strength:	60

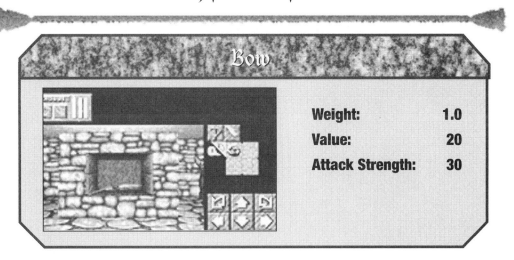

Bow

Weight:	1.0
Value:	20
Attack Strength:	30

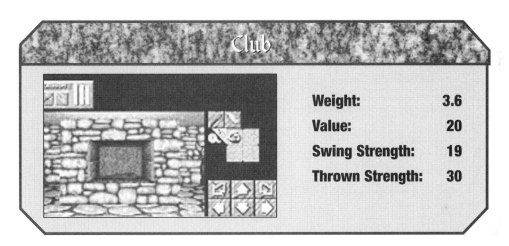

Club

Weight:	3.6
Value:	20
Swing Strength:	19
Thrown Strength:	30

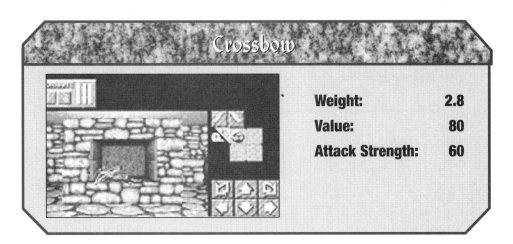

Crossbow

Weight:	2.8
Value:	80
Attack Strength:	60

Dagger

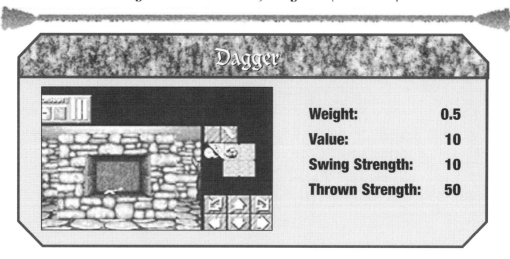

Weight:	0.5
Value:	10
Swing Strength:	10
Thrown Strength:	50

Poison Dart

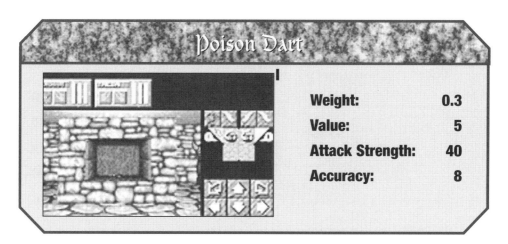

Weight:	0.3
Value:	5
Attack Strength:	40
Accuracy:	8

Katana

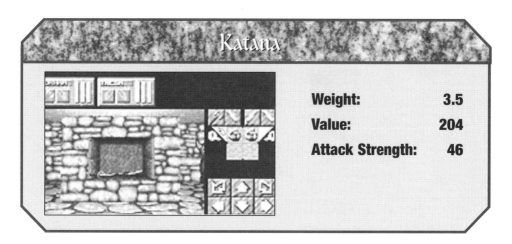

Weight:	3.5
Value:	204
Attack Strength:	46

Mace

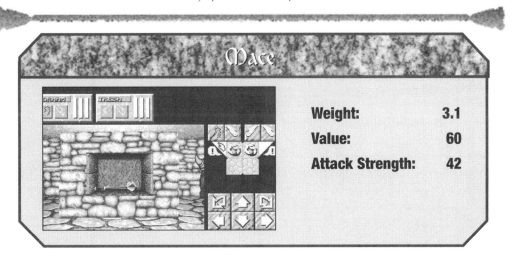

Weight:	3.1
Value:	60
Attack Strength:	42

Machete

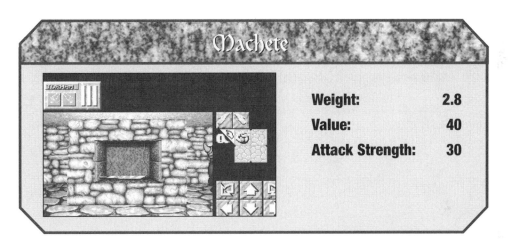

Weight:	2.8
Value:	40
Attack Strength:	30

Morning Star

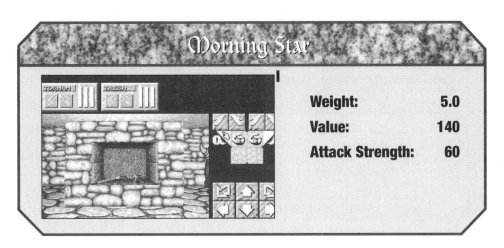

Weight:	5.0
Value:	140
Attack Strength:	60

Rock

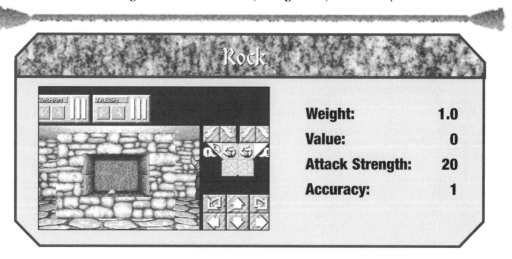

Weight:	1.0
Value:	0
Attack Strength:	20
Accuracy:	1

Sabre

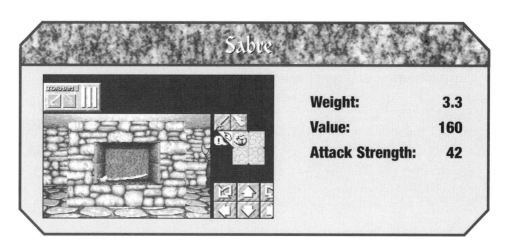

Weight:	3.3
Value:	160
Attack Strength:	42

Scythe

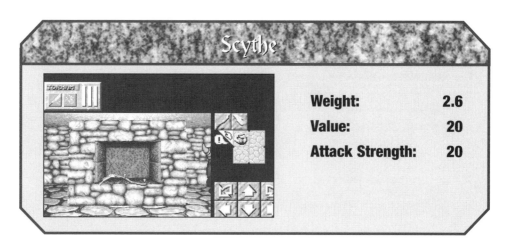

Weight:	2.6
Value:	20
Attack Strength:	20

War Club

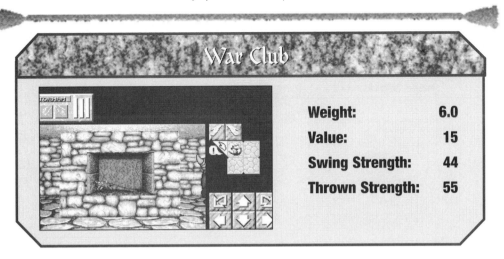

Weight:	6.0
Value:	15
Swing Strength:	44
Thrown Strength:	55

Sling

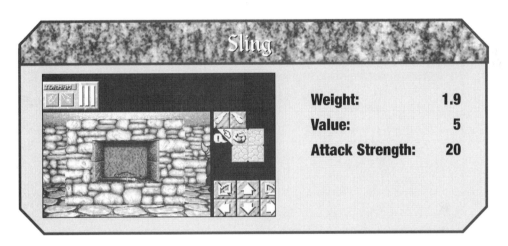

Weight:	1.9
Value:	5
Attack Strength:	20

Slayer Arrow

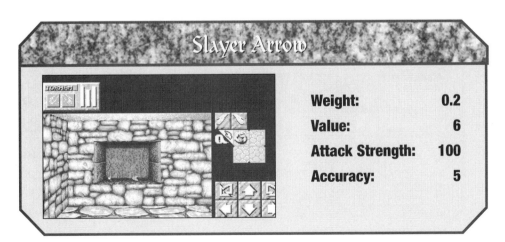

Weight:	0.2
Value:	6
Attack Strength:	100
Accuracy:	5

Speedbow

Weight:	3.0
Value:	180
Attack Strength:	90

Stick

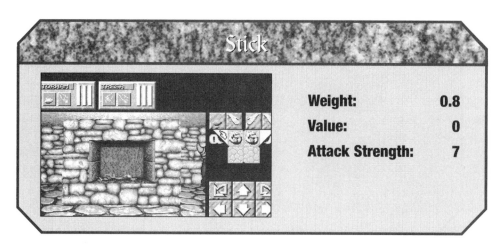

Weight:	0.8
Value:	0
Attack Strength:	7

Sword

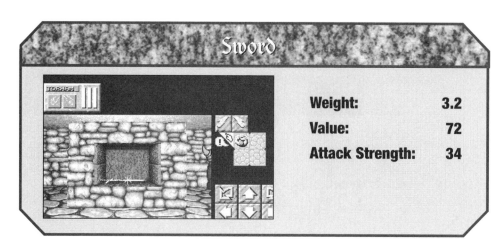

Weight:	3.2
Value:	72
Attack Strength:	34

Tech Mace

Weight:	4.1
Value:	376
Attack Strength:	65

Shuriken

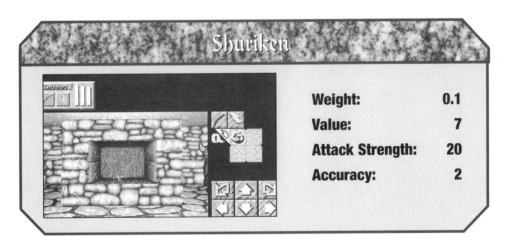

Weight:	0.1
Value:	7
Attack Strength:	20
Accuracy:	2

Torch

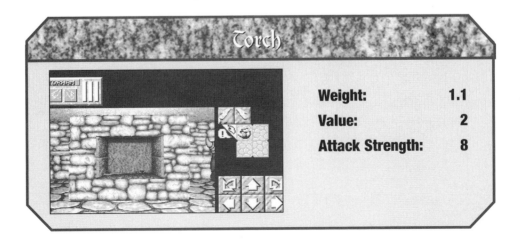

Weight:	1.1
Value:	2
Attack Strength:	8

Vorax

Weight:	6.5
Value:	660
Attack Strength:	70

NOTES:

This is a much better version of the standard ax, inflicting far more damage.

Vorpal Blade

Weight	3.0
Value:	400
Attack Strength:	48

NOTES:

The Vorpal Blade allows the user to disrupt opponents. While not inherently magickal, this blade is one of the only things that will damage certain creatures, and, thus, is a good weapon to have handy.

ZO Blade

Weight:	1.0
Value:	900
Attack Strength:	45

NOTES:

This blade is not metal but is actually a rent in the fabric of space and time. It doesn't cut the opposition but instead sends a small slice of them into nowhere.

Armor

The only major problem with having plenty of weapons is the potential for other creatures to have plenty of weapons also. To this end, it's wise for even the most macho hero to be fully conversant in protective equipment.

The following list is a complete index of all those protective devices in the realm of a non-magickal nature.

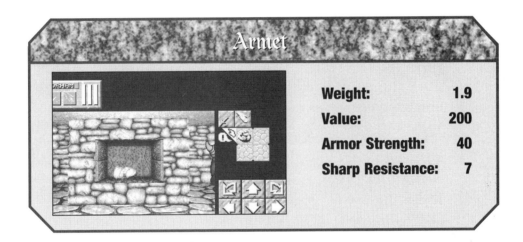

Armet	
Weight:	1.9
Value:	200
Armor Strength:	40
Sharp Resistance:	7

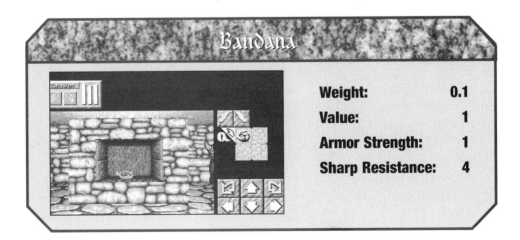

Bandana	
Weight:	0.1
Value:	1
Armor Strength:	1
Sharp Resistance:	4

Black Top

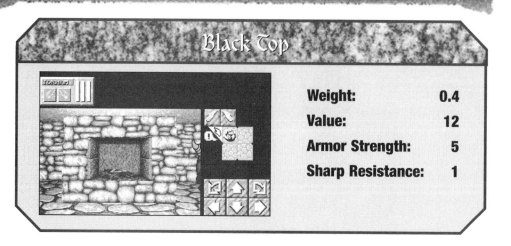

Weight:	0.4
Value:	12
Armor Strength:	5
Sharp Resistance:	1

Bodice

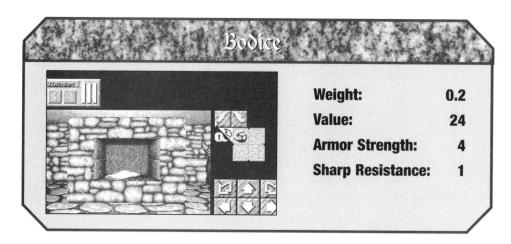

Weight:	0.2
Value:	24
Armor Strength:	4
Sharp Resistance:	1

Blue Pants

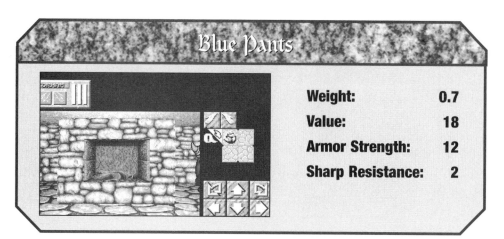

Weight:	0.7
Value:	18
Armor Strength:	12
Sharp Resistance:	2

Breastplate

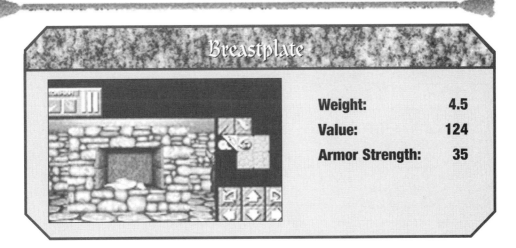

Weight:	4.5
Value:	124
Armor Strength:	35

Brigandine

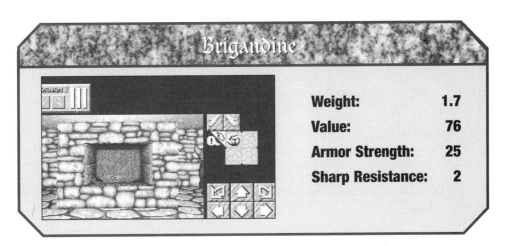

Weight:	1.7
Value:	76
Armor Strength:	25
Sharp Resistance:	2

Bascinet

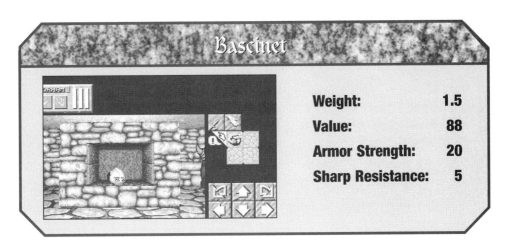

Weight:	1.5
Value:	88
Armor Strength:	20
Sharp Resistance:	5

Cape

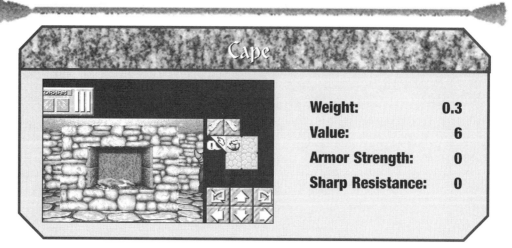

Weight:	0.3
Value:	6
Armor Strength:	0
Sharp Resistance:	0

Doublet

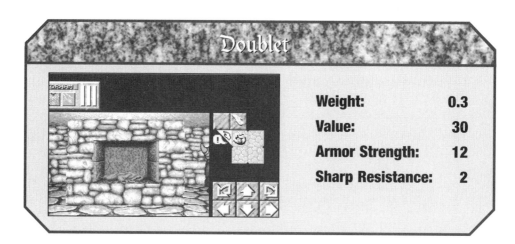

Weight:	0.3
Value:	30
Armor Strength:	12
Sharp Resistance:	2

Foot Plate

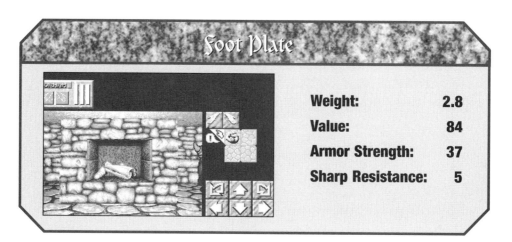

Weight:	2.8
Value:	84
Armor Strength:	37
Sharp Resistance:	5

Fire Plate

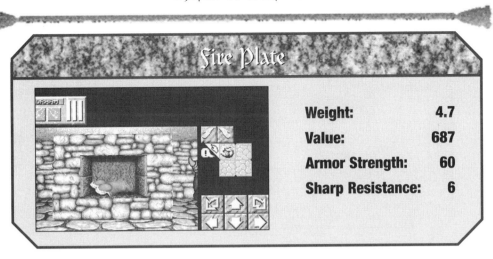

Weight:	4.7
Value:	687
Armor Strength:	60
Sharp Resistance:	6

Fire Greave

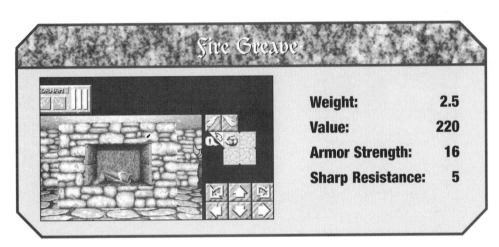

Weight:	2.5
Value:	220
Armor Strength:	16
Sharp Resistance:	5

Fire Plate

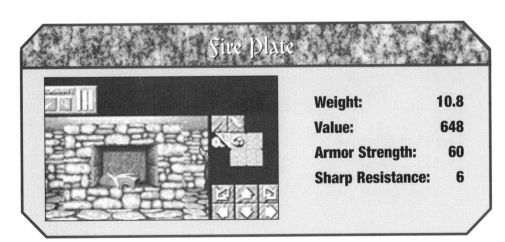

Weight:	10.8
Value:	648
Armor Strength:	60
Sharp Resistance:	6

Greaves

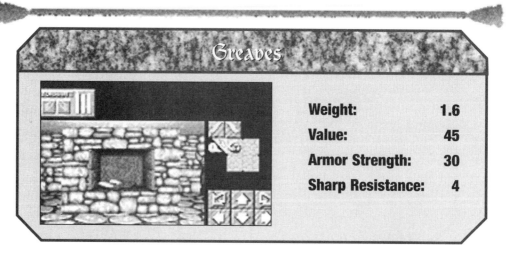

Weight:	1.6
Value:	45
Armor Strength:	30
Sharp Resistance:	4

Great Helm

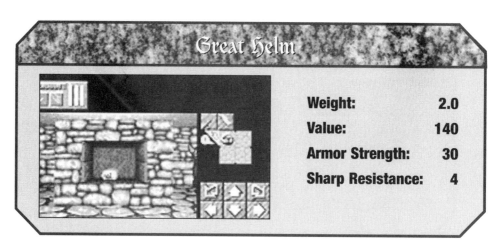

Weight:	2.0
Value:	140
Armor Strength:	30
Sharp Resistance:	4

Gunna

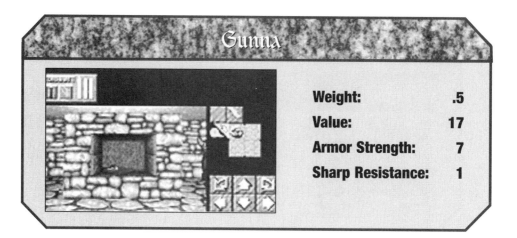

Weight:	.5
Value:	17
Armor Strength:	7
Sharp Resistance:	1

Helmet

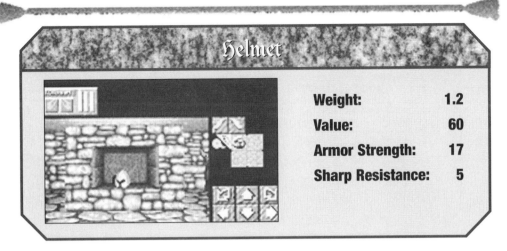

Weight:	1.2
Value:	60
Armor Strength:	17
Sharp Resistance:	5

Horned Helm

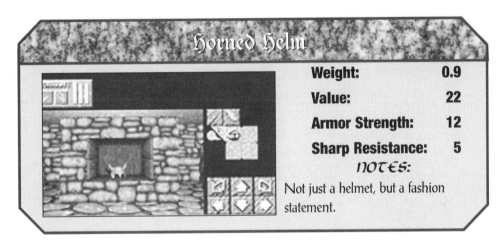

Weight:	0.9
Value:	22
Armor Strength:	12
Sharp Resistance:	5

NOTES:

Not just a helmet, but a fashion statement.

Huke

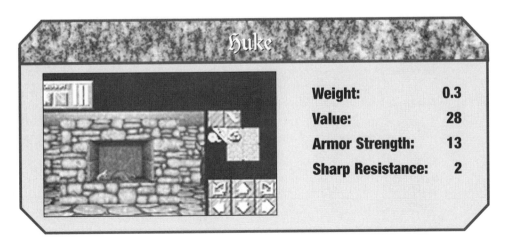

Weight:	0.3
Value:	28
Armor Strength:	13
Sharp Resistance:	2

Leather Boots

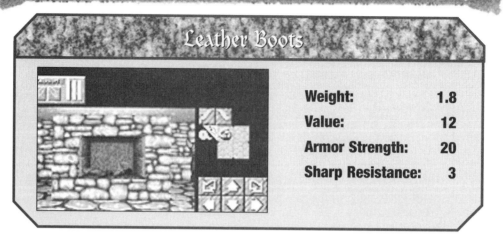

Weight:	1.8
Value:	12
Armor Strength:	20
Sharp Resistance:	3

Leather Jerkin

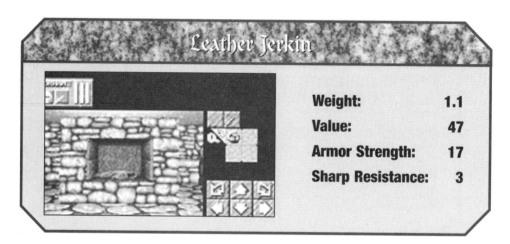

Weight:	1.1
Value:	47
Armor Strength:	17
Sharp Resistance:	3

Leather Pants

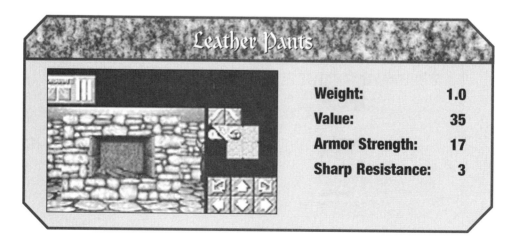

Weight:	1.0
Value:	35
Armor Strength:	17
Sharp Resistance:	3

Mail Helmet

Weight:	1.6
Value:	42
Armor Strength:	30
Sharp Resistance:	5

Mithral Huke

Weight:	4.1
Value:	260
Armor Strength:	60
Sharp Resistance:	5

Mithral Mail

Weight:	5.2
Value:	352
Armor Strength:	70
Sharp Resistance:	5

Fine Robe Top

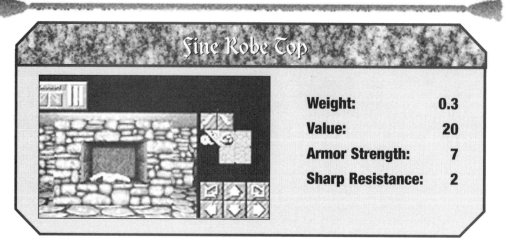

Weight:	0.3
Value:	20
Armor Strength:	7
Sharp Resistance:	2

Fine Robe Bottom

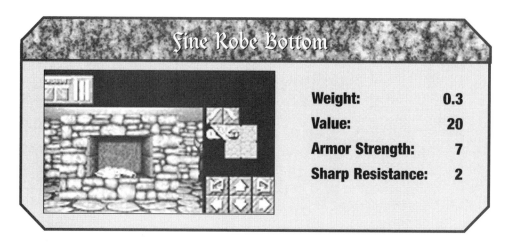

Weight:	0.3
Value:	20
Armor Strength:	7
Sharp Resistance:	2

RA SAR GReaves

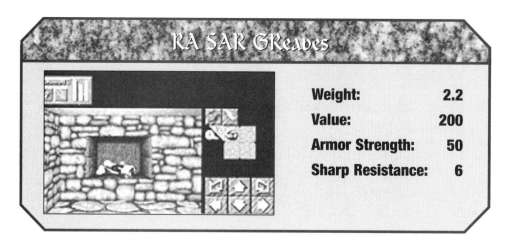

Weight:	2.2
Value:	200
Armor Strength:	50
Sharp Resistance:	6

RA SAR Poleyn

Weight:	6.2
Value:	400
Armor Strength:	90
Sharp Resistance:	6

Sandals

Weight:	0.6
Value:	3
Armor Strength:	4
Sharp Resistance:	1

Scale Hauberk

Weight:	5.4
Value:	160
Armor Strength:	45
Sharp Resistance:	4

Scale Mail

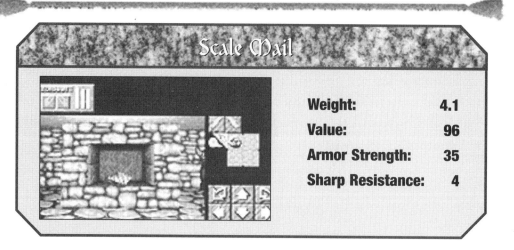

Weight:	4.1
Value:	96
Armor Strength:	35
Sharp Resistance:	4

Small Shield

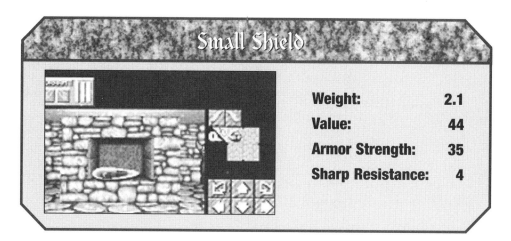

Weight:	2.1
Value:	44
Armor Strength:	35
Sharp Resistance:	4

Tabard

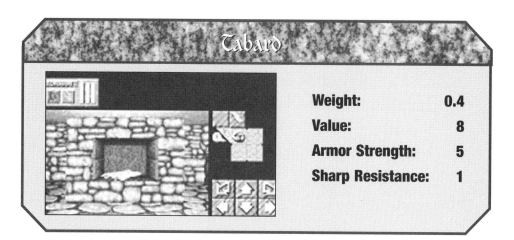

Weight:	0.4
Value:	8
Armor Strength:	5
Sharp Resistance:	1

Tech Boots

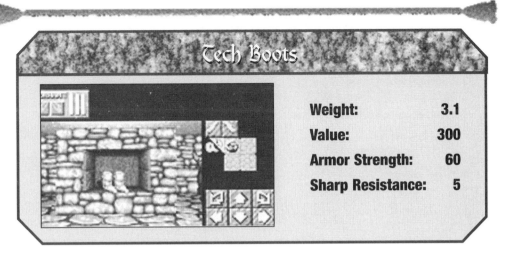

Weight:	3.1
Value:	300
Armor Strength:	60
Sharp Resistance:	5

Tech Poleyn

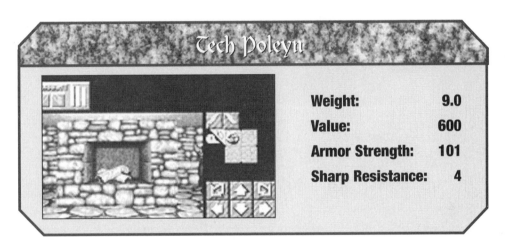

Weight:	9.0
Value:	600
Armor Strength:	101
Sharp Resistance:	4

Thigh Plates

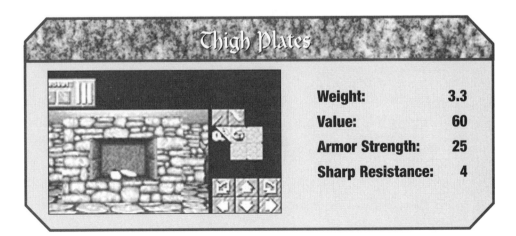

Weight:	3.3
Value:	60
Armor Strength:	25
Sharp Resistance:	4

Torso Plate

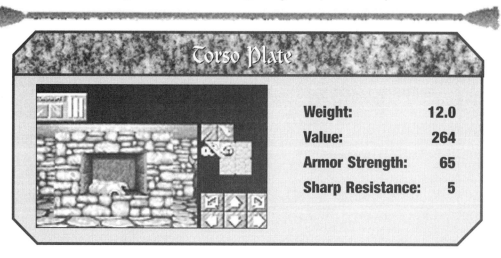

Weight:	12.0
Value:	264
Armor Strength:	65
Sharp Resistance:	5

Tunic

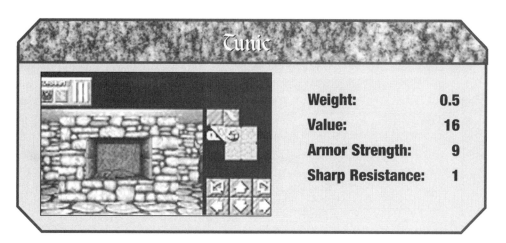

Weight:	0.5
Value:	16
Armor Strength:	9
Sharp Resistance:	1

Wood Shield

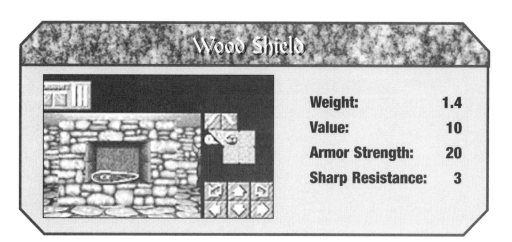

Weight:	1.4
Value:	10
Armor Strength:	20
Sharp Resistance:	3

SAR Shield

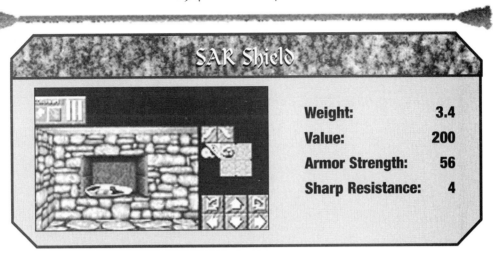

Weight:	3.4
Value:	200
Armor Strength:	56
Sharp Resistance:	4

Leg Plates

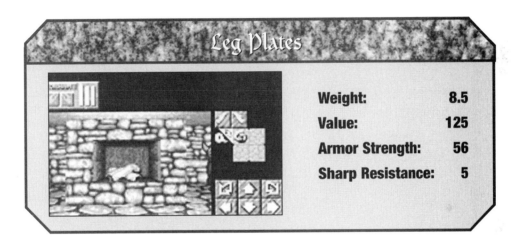

Weight:	8.5
Value:	125
Armor Strength:	56
Sharp Resistance:	5

The Ugly Bits

ow for the ugly bits," said Tanic, as we all clustered about the sun key door, wasting time, being briefed or catching up on our tans, depending on your point of view.

"The defenses that have been set up to guard the Zo Link are going to work against us now."

I stifled a yawn.

"This means that we are going to have to pass through the locked areas leading to the parts of the Zo Link. We must find a key or solve a puzzle in each area in order to go on to the next one."

Tanic's voice started to rise, and his eyes started to glow with that peculiar inner fire possessed only by true heroes or the severely mentally unbalanced. Now that I think about it, the former is really a subset of the latter.

Anyhow, with his voice rising like a Priest on a roll, he continued.

"Think of each of these areas as a challenge. Not as a drudgery or a trap, but as a way to prove ourselves! A...a..."

"Quest!" supplied Ravenblood, smirking at me.

"Yes, a quest!" Tanic resumed. "That's just the thing! So let's march smartly on to complete our first quest!"

He rose and jutted his chin out at what must have been a heroic angle. Then, with a flourish, he started to turn the key in the door.

"Er, excuse me," said Ravenblood.

Tanic looked back, annoyed.

"What is it?" he asked.

Ravenblood nudged me in the ribs.

"Second quest, don't you mean?"

Tanic stared at him.

"Eh?"

"Well, you said we had to get out of each locked area, and to think of each one as a quest, right?"

I could tell Ravenblood was having a problem keeping a straight face.

"Yes, what of it?"

"Then this impending quest would be the second one. First one would be getting out of this area, now wouldn't it?"

"Well, we didn't do all that much here."

"Doesn't matter. You make a numbering system, you have to stick to it. Can you see the historians later? What are they going to call the killing of the glops in the courtyard, now? The pre-quest? An introduction?"

I suddenly realized that if this went on long enough, we would have to retire to the pubs to argue the issue.

"I agree with Ravenblood. We owe it to future generations to get this thing right, numerically speaking," I said.

Tanic was getting seriously perturbed.

"Well, then, it is the second quest we are going on. Now, with that settled, let's move forward on the second quest!"

He started reaching for the key again.

"Uh, excuse me," I said.

"What?!"

"Well, I am just wondering if this bit here should really count. You know? I mean, I am thinking that the door was locked from this side, more to keep things out. Particularly if you think about the fact that we found the key on this side, right there on the table."

"And what difference would that make?" Tanic asked.

"Well, in that case, this bit really wouldn't be a quest at all, and we should only count the bits between two locked doors. So this would be our first quest. I mean it isn't a great accomplishment if you unlock your house door in the morning to go out, now is it?"

Tanic was struggling to follow this.

"So you are saying this should be the first quest."

"Exactly."

"Right, then. Here we go. On to the first quest!"

With a great flourish he started to turn the key.

"No, now this just won't work at all," said Ravenblood.

"What's the problem now!" Tanic was practically screaming at this point.

"Well, let's think this 'only between two locked doors' thing all the way out. What about the last bit, eh! You know, sooner or later we are going to have to fight in a room at the end, you can't have a universe made up of infinite locked doors, now can you!"

I shook my head solemnly.

"Well, there you go," Ravenblood continued. "Sooner or later we are going to have to fight in a place with no locked door on the other side. What then, eh! Probably some great heroic battle, and it doesn't count as a quest at all. Not between two locked doors, you see."

"So what is your point!" The veins on Tanic's neck were bulging.

"I would say the quest we are going on is, in point of fact, our second quest."

Tanic couldn't speak all that well at this point. He just nodded his head and started to turn the key.

I cleared my throat to speak.

Tanic let out an inarticulate scream of rage and spun on me, pulling his sword. He stuck it out with the point nary an inch from my chest.

"I was just going to say, second quest it is then, eh!" I gave him a quick, if weak, smile.

Finally, he managed to turn the key and push the door open.

We marched carefully into the thicket on the other side. Tanic was looking to the left and right, jutting his jaw first one way and then the other, making sure that no matter what angle you viewed him from, you would catch his most heroic side at least half of the time.

However, he looked much less heroic when a good sized worm-like thing poked it's head out of the ground and sucked his foot into its maw.

"Worms!" he screamed, and started hacking at the ground with his sword. The worm, knowing the wrong end of a sword blade when it saw one point blank, decided to go back underground. Of course, it tried to take Tanic's foot with it. Tanic stumbled as his foot was pulled into a hole.

Tanic kept poking the sword into the ground, and Zilch started looking around and rapidly found another worm trying to blindside us from from behind a thicket. He just punched it, and the worm recoiled.

"Nice trees, wouldn't you say!" Ravenblood asked me.

"Tis a beautiful view," I agreed.

Suddenly a worm sprouted out of the ground to Ravenblood's left and lunged for him.

I fumbled for my runes, and I could see that Ravenblood was doing the same.

A worm hit me from the side, I felt fire shoot up my left thigh.

Zilch, up front, was still swinging like a champion, but Tanic was looking a bit the worse for wear. Ravenblood took a couple of hits from his worm and dropped his rune bag. As he reached down to pick it up, he took a hit to the arm.

We were getting mangled.

"Retreat!" I screamed, and started running for the door back to the shops.

Ravenblood was right on my heels, and, I was surprised to note, Tanic was bringing up the rear without hesitation.

We made it through the door and I realized that Zilch wasn't with us.

"Dung!" I spat. "We have to go back for Zilch."

I stuck my head back through the door and yelled at him at the top of my voice.

"Zilch, retreat!"

He kept swinging.

I thought about it for a second.

"That means run away!" I added.

Zilch was still duking it out with the digger worms.

I grabbed Ravenblood by the collar and hauled him back in to help get Zilch.

Without much coordination, Ravenblood hooked Zilch's legs with his staff and I clipped the giant neatly behind the ear with the butt of my dagger as he fell. Then each of us grabbed a leg and hauled him back through the gate.

> THE IMPORTANCE OF THE STRATEGIC RETREAT CANNOT BE UNDERESTIMATED. AS POINTED OUT BEFORE, HEROES GET TIME TO HEAL UP, BUT THE MONSTERS DO NOT. ALSO, IF AN ADVENTURER FALLS DURING COMBAT, IT IS A GREAT EFFORT TO COLLECT THEIR BODY AND EQUIPMENT WHILE DEALING WITH THE ENEMY. DURING ALL CONFLICTS, ALWAYS MAKE SURE THAT YOUR PARTY MEMBERS AREN'T TAKING TOO MUCH DAMAGE.

Zilch snored on the ground as we tended our wounds, moaning now and then as a particularly tender spot was mended.

"Oh, we'll just eat digger worms," I said sarcastically.

"They are a bit slimy but edible."

Tanic just looked sullen.

"I think that is more the digger worm's line, don't you!" Ravenblood said. "Those humans aren't the best food, but one of them is good for a quick bite.'"

"A minor setback," mumbled Tanic.

"Look, let's sleep on it and figure it all out in the morning," I said. "Then we'll make another go at it."

Tanic looked at his foot, which was swelling quite a bit, and nodded his head. Then he spread his bedroll and lay down.

"I think I might need a few more supplies," said Ravenblood getting up to head for the settlement.

"Me too," I agreed.

Ravenblood tossed a healing potion to the supine Tanic on our way out.

In the pub, we discussed the situation.

"Well, this just isn't going to work," he said as he finished a great draught of ale.

"There has to be some way of doing it. There wouldn't be ballads of great heroes if the average hero was getting mauled by digger worms right out of the gate."

He looked at me sourly and took a bite of thorn demon steak.

"No, there has to be a way," I said. "Let's look at what we did wrong."

I held up one finger.

"First, you and I didn't help. Now I realize that didn't seem such a problem at first, but then we got surrounded. From now on we are going to have to jump in with spells right from the get-go. I mean, we could get hurt here."

I held up another finger.

"Second, we need to have our runes ready when things get ugly. You saw how even when we get attacked we don't do so well at getting our spells prepared on the fly. This isn't some magickal academy class we are dealing with here. These are demonic monsters."

PLAN ATTACKS THAT WILL DO AS MUCH DAMAGE AS POSSIBLE BY PREPARING SPELLS LIKE fIREBALLS IN ADVANCE. AT POINT-BLANK RANGE, MONSTERS WON'T HAVE THE TIME TO STEP OUT OF THE WAY OF SUCH A SPELL. FIREBALLS ARE PARTICULARLY WELL SUITED TO COMBAT NOT ONLY BECAUSE OF THEIR DAMAGE, BUT ALSO BECAUSE THE SYLLABLES MAKING UP THE SPELL, EE, FUL AND IR, ARE ALL ON THE SAME LINE. THIS MEANS THAT WHEN YOU CAN CAST MULTIPLES OF THE SPELL AT HIGHER LEVELS, fIREBALLS ARE QUICK TO CREATE IN THE HEAT OF BATTLE. ALSO, THEY DO A GREAT DEAL OF DAMAGE TO MONSTERS COMPARED TO NORMAL WEAPONS. VERY FEW MONSTERS CAN WITHSTAND A BARRAGE OF THESE fIREBALLS PREPARED BEFORE A BATTLE.

THE BASIC STRATEGY SHOULD BE "HIT AND RUN." PREPARE THE SPELLS BEFORE BATTLE, fIREBALL THE MONSTERS RIGHT OFF THE BAT, HACK THEM A FEW TIMES WITH MELEE WEAPONS AND THEN HIT THEM WITH ANY ADDITIONAL SPELLS IF THE CASTERS HAVE ENOUGH MANA TO CAST AGAIN. THEN RUN AWAY, SLEEP TO RESTORE MANA, AND RETURN TO fINISH THE JOB.

I held up a third finger.

"Last, we need to keep moving. We were just standing there. Obviously, if we do that we are going to be monster food. If we manage to keep moving and cast and attack at the same time, then we might really be able to do something impressive."

> THE BEST METHOD OF FIGHTING AND MOVING IS TO USE BOTH THE MOUSE AND THE KEYBOARD AT THE SAME TIME. SINCE YOU CAN ONLY GIVE ONE COMMAND AT A TIME WITH THE POINTER, REPOSITIONING THE POINTER TO THE MOVEMENT ICONS MEANS NO ATTACKS. YOU CAN MANEUVER WITH ONE HAND ON THE ARROW KEYS WHILE USING THE OTHER HAND ON THE MOUSE TO CONTROL THE ATTACKS. THIS EFFECTIVELY DOUBLES YOUR RATE OF FIRE WHILE ADVANCING, SIDESTEPPING, OR RETREATING. IT TAKES A BIT OF PRACTICE TO MASTER, BUT THE INHERENT ADVANTAGES ARE OBVIOUS.

Ravenblood was none too impressed, but in the morning I outlined our plan to the rest of the party, and off we went to complete the second quest.

The glops vaporized with the first fireball barrage, and I was beaming.

The digger worms fell to our moving might and magick show. I patted myself on the back.

The thorn demons mauled us so badly we were lucky to get out without anyone dead.

That night, in the pub with Ravenblood, I held up four fingers.

"Fourth, know when to fight. Those worms weren't all that fast, if we had just run right through them we might have been able to make it."

> NOT ONLY IS IT PARAMOUNT TO UNDERSTAND WHEN TO RUN AWAY, IT IS ALSO IMPORTANT TO KNOW WHEN NOT TO FIGHT AT ALL. AT LOWER LEVELS, THE THORN DEMONS AND WOLVES IN PARTICULAR HAVE THE POTENTIAL TO EAT AN ENTIRE PARTY OF YOUNG ADVENTURERS AND NOT MISS A BEAT. HENCE, SIMPLY DON'T ATTACK THEM.
>
> IN MANY CASES, A PARTY CAN RUN AROUND A GROUP OF OFFENDING CREATURES. HOWEVER, WITH SOME TYPES OF MONSTERS, A STALWART PARTY CAN WALK RIGHT THROUGH THEM. THORN DEMONS AND WOLVES ARE PARTICULARLY UNINTERESTED IN THE MOVEMENTS OF RANDOM ADVENTURERS AND, IF UNMOLESTED, WILL OFTEN ALLOW THE SMART PARTY TO SIMPLY WALK THROUGH THEIR RANKS. HOWEVER, IT IS PARAMOUNT NOT TO ENGAGE THE CREATURES, FOR THIS WILL BRING THE WRATH OF ALL OF THEM. FROM TIME TO TIME, SOME MINOR HITS WILL BE TAKEN AS THE ODD WOLF OR THORN DEMON ATTACKS THE PARTY, BUT IGNORING THE ATTACK WILL OFTEN STOP A FULL-FLEDGED FIGHT.
>
> SINCE DUNGEON MASTER II IS A REAL-TIME GAME, RUNNING IS A GOOD IDEA. THE LESS TIME EXPOSED TO A THREAT, THE BETTER.

Ravenblood protested for a while, but, with a bit more ale and effort, he agreed that we could become regular killing machines and left the pub confident, if wobbling.

The next day we set off again. And right past the door we ran into the worms. Two fireballs made short work of them. I smiled and we continued on.

A group of glops, however, proved a slight problem, in that we killed them too quickly.

"Well, I think we are ready to get some of those thorn demon steaks, what say you all!" Tanic said happily as he cleaned the last of the glops off his blade.

"Er, they look a bit large," I said.

"And tough," said Ravenblood.

"Are we heroes, or wimps!" Tanic asked rhetorically as he strode toward a field with a few thorn demons milling about.

We stopped just within spell range.

"Okay. One, two, three, duck!" I shouted as I prepared and hurled a fireball from the back rank. With a now practiced motion, Tanic and Zilch ducked as my fireball whizzed over their heads. Ravenblood's much smaller fireball was right behind mine.

They both hit the lead thorn demon, and he looked up from his shrub chewing. For a moment it looked like he was going to go back to chewing and just ignore the best fireballs we could throw at him. Then he charged.

"Duck!" I yelled, as Ravenblood and I hurled our darts.

The poison darts, which had been so effective with the glops and digger worms, just stuck in the thick hide of the thorn demon. This was starting to look bad.

Then the thing was upon us.

We danced to the left and to the right. Tanic and Zilch hacked heroically, but soon we were getting mauled pretty badly.

Tanic called retreat and started to backpedal.

Ravenblood and I knew our cue. He went low and I went high, and soon we were dragging the unconscious Zilch at high speed out of the thicket and back to the door.

Back in the shop area, we tended our wounds. By now running away was getting to be old hat, and no one seemed very upset that we hadn't won this round.

"Those darts aren't worth much." I muttered.

"Not against anything more dangerous than a poodle," Ravenblood agreed wearily.

WHEN FIGHTING THE DIGGER WORMS OR GLOPS, THE USE OF THE BACK RANK CHARACTERS TO HURL POISON DARTS OR DAGGERS IS EFFECTIVE. HOWEVER, WITH ANY BIGGER PREY, THE TIME SPENT HURLING THE WEAPONS ISN'T WORTH IT. THE WEAPONS STAY IN THE CREATURE UNTIL IT IS KILLED, AND THE SMALLER WEAPONS DON'T DO AN APPRECIABLE AMOUNT OF DAMAGE. INSTEAD, USE THE TIME THAT IT WOULD TAKE TO COMMAND THOSE CHARACTERS TO THROW THEIR WEAPONS TO BEGIN A FIGHTING MELEE WITH THE FRONT RANK CHARACTERS.

THE SAME TIME LOSS IS OFTEN CRUCIAL IN TURNING INDIVIDUAL CHARACTERS TO FIGHT TO THE SIDES. WHILE THE BACK RANK CHARACTERS CAN BE TURNED TO THE SIDES OF THE PARTY TO FIGHT, THIS ACTION IS TIME CONSUMING. IT IS ALMOST ALWAYS MORE EFFECTIVE JUST TO MAKE THE WHOLE PARTY FACE IN THAT DIRECTION AND USE THE GAINED TIME TO MAKE A COUPLE OF EXTRA ATTACKS.

After a good sleep (and a few pints of ale), we made another run at the thorn demons.

When we got in range, I yelled "duck." Tanic and Zilch dropped to one knee and my fireball belched from the air and flew over their heads. Ravenblood's, however, didn't. Instead, a faint glow suffused us all.

"And what the heck was that?" I asked, as we ran up to let Zilch and Tanic slash on the hapless thorn demon, who still had our darts sticking out of its hide. Apparently it hadn't noticed them or bothered to pull them out. Maybe darts in the hide were a fashion statement among thorn demons.

"Protection spell," Ravenblood replied.

"Fool. Waste of good mana. We are probably going to have to make another run at this now."

He bristled.

"What do you mean?" he asked.

"Have you noticed that we aren't getting hit? Ever since we started staying light on our feet, we just aren't taking any real damage. So you waste mana on some stupid Priest spell when we could have given the thorn demon another fireball!" I spat.

PROTECTION SPELLS EFFECTIVELY BLOCK SOME OF THE DAMAGE OF ATTACKS COMING INTO THE PARTY. HOWEVER, ONCE THE MOVEMENT PATTERNS OF THE MONSTERS ARE SEEN, IT IS ALMOST ALWAYS A BETTER IDEA TO USE THE MANA TO CAST FIREBALLS. THE REASON HAS TO DO WITH THE SPEED OF THE MONSTERS.

IN THE LOWER LEVELS, MONSTERS ARE SLOW. THORN DEMONS, FOR EXAMPLE, RAISE THEIR CLAWS BEFORE THEY SWIPE AT THE CHARACTERS, GIVING TIME FOR A QUICK PLAYER TO MOVE THE PARTY BACK BEFORE THE ATTACK LANDS.

HIGHER LEVEL MONSTERS ARE FAST ENOUGH TO HIT BEFORE THE PARTY CAN BE MOVED OUT OF THE WAY, BUT BY THE TIME THE HIGHER LEVEL MONSTERS ARE ENCOUNTERED, THE PARTY HAS ACQUIRED ENOUGH EXPERIENCE AND EQUIPMENT THAT IT CAN EFFECTIVELY TAKE THE DAMAGE. SOME PLAYERS, PARTICULARLY THOSE WITH A BIT LESS DEXTERITY, MIGHT WISH TO EXPERIMENT WITH PROTECTION SPELLS, BUT IN GENERAL IT IS A BETTER PRACTICE TO FORGO THESE INCANTATIONS IN FAVOR OF CAUSING MORE DAMAGE TO THE CREATURE IN QUESTION. WITH THE RETREAT-AND-RETURN STRATEGY, USING ALL DAMAGE SPELLS PROVES MUCH MORE EFFECTIVE IN PRACTICE.

Our arguing was cut short, however, by Tanic calling retreat. Ravenblood and I performed what we had taken to calling the Zilch Maneuver, and hauled him out with us.

On the third run we had to retreat again.

And on the fourth.

As we were sitting around resting up from the fourth run, we discussed our distressing lack of progress.

"I don't see how they sell thorn demon steaks at all," said Ravenblood. "If it takes this much to kill them, the things should be worth 50 coppers a piece. We have to be making a mistake of some sort."

"Well, I think we will get it this time," said Tanic, leaning against a wall and sharpening his sword.

"Those things are unbelievably tough. A wonder you can eat the meat," I mumbled.

"Different," rumbled Zilch.

"What?" Tanic asked him.

"Different," repeated Zilch.

I mulled this over.

"I think he is saying that we aren't hitting the same thorn demon."

"No," said Ravenblood with a sinking voice.

"You know, I was thinking the spots on that last one might have looked different. But I figured it was the light," I said.

"Then we are going to have to keep this up until we luck out and find the one we hit before!" Ravenblood asked.

"Guess so. Once a hero starts a job he doesn't back down," Tanic said.

There was much grumbling about this as we went to sleep.

On the next run, we finally killed one. But since we went over the carcass with a fine tooth comb and didn't find our darts, it was obvious that we had indeed been fighting a number of different thorn demons. But we had to get the darts back.

THE ONLY DRAWBACK WITH THE HIT AND RUN STRATEGY IS THE INABILITY TO BE POSITIVE THAT THE RIGHT CREATURE IS BEING TARGETED OUT OF A CROWD. IN MOST CASES YOU ARE TRYING TO KILL THEM ALL ANYWAY, BUT IN SOME LIMITED INSTANCES, LIKE WHEN YOU ARE DEALING WITH THORN DEMONS, THIS PROVES TO BE A DRAWBACK, PARTICULARLY IN RETRIEVING ANYTHING THAT HAS BEEN SUNK INTO ONE OF THE CREATURES. BUT AT THE LEVEL WHERE THIS IS A PROBLEM, THE PARTY NEEDS THE EXPERIENCE ANYWAY, AND EVERY EXTRA MONSTER KILLED HELPS ADVANCE THE SKILLS OF THE CHAMPIONS.

It took five more runs before we finally killed the one with the darts in him.

After we retrieved the darts, we stopped to practice some more. It turned out that many of the things I had done in battle, and seen Zilch and Tanic do, rubbed off. I started to get pretty handy with the darts.

KEEP DOING STATIC PRACTICE AGAINST TREES OR DOORS, AND WORKING WITH SPELLS BETWEEN FIGHTING. WHILE IT IS BORING TO JUST STAND AROUND PRACTICING, IT SOLIDIFIES THE SKILLS LEARNED DURING COMBAT AND IMPROVES THE OVERALL PERFORMANCE OF THE PARTY. LEVEL PROGRESSION IS GREATLY INCREASED WITH PRACTICE AS OPPOSED TO JUST FIGHTING CONTINUOUSLY. ALSO, THE FRONT LINE FIGHTERS DON'T GET MUCH OF A CHANCE TO CAST MANY SPELLS DURING THE AVERAGE COMBAT, BUT JUST BY SEEING SPELLS CAST THEY ARE GIVEN SOME GOOD IDEAS. EMPHASIZING THIS WITH PRACTICE ALLOWS THEM TO GAIN SKILL LEVELS IN CLASSES THAT THEY AREN'T ACTUALLY USING DURING COMBAT.

Finally, with our bellies full of steaks, it was time to continue with our "quests."

Maps and Stuff

Level Overviews

These maps show the overall view of each level. The levels run from 8, which is underground, up to 1, the roof of the castle. Level 6 is ground level.

Level 8

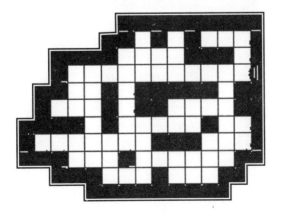

131

Level 7

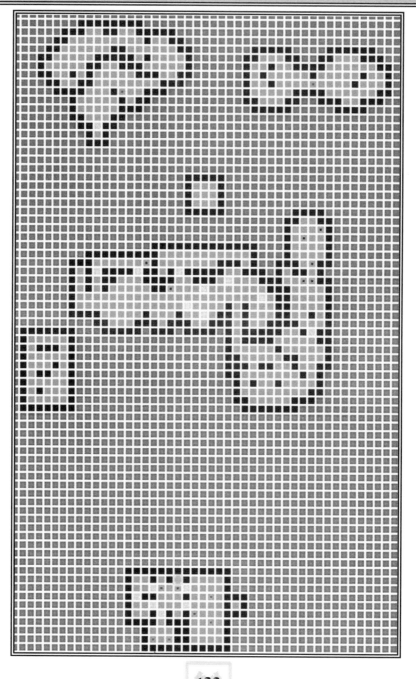

Level 6 (Ground Level)

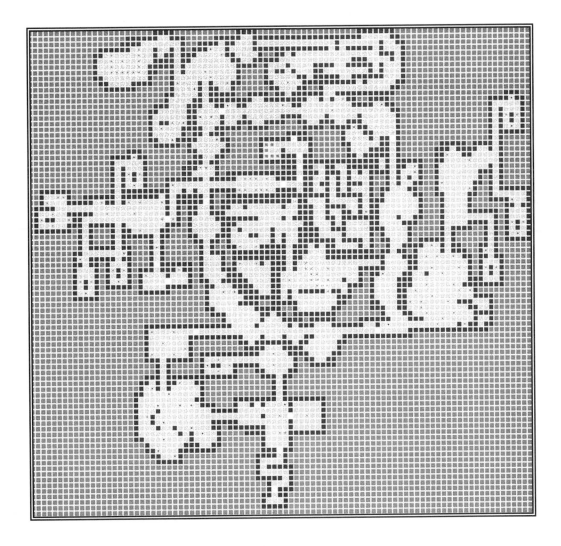

Level 5

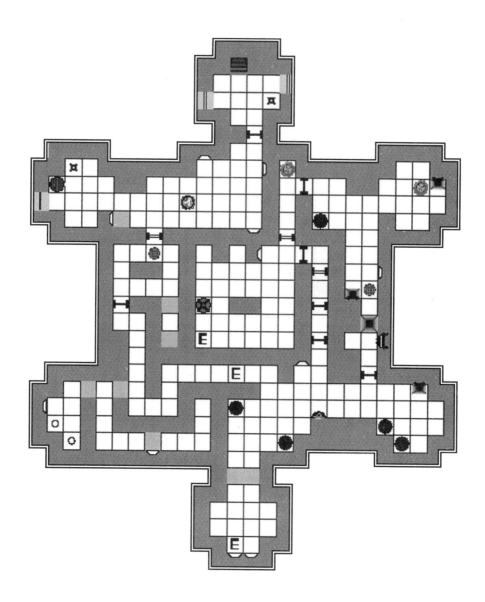

Level 4

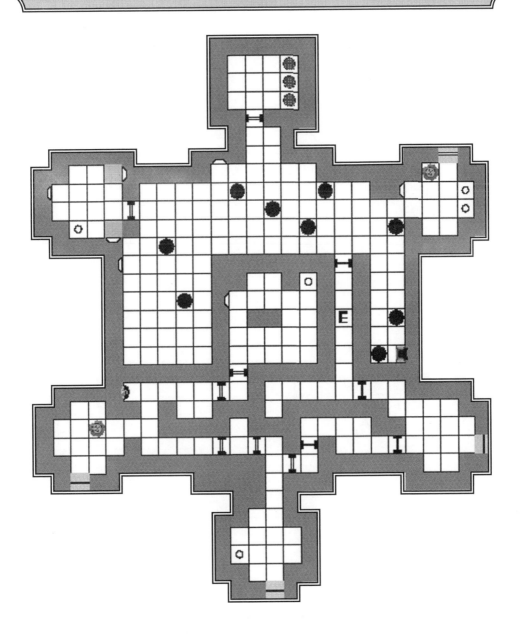

Level 3

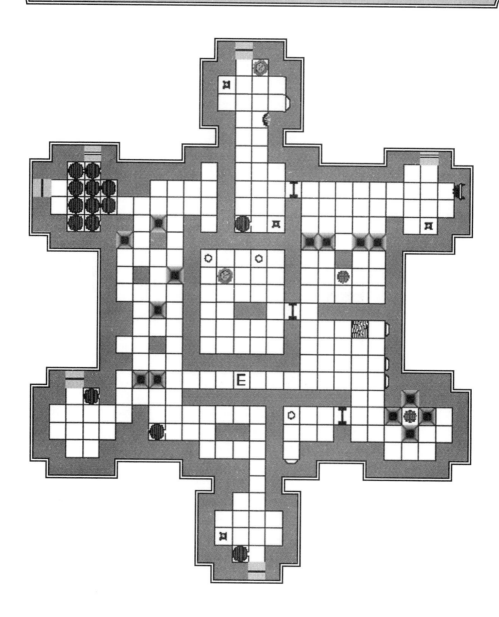

Level 2

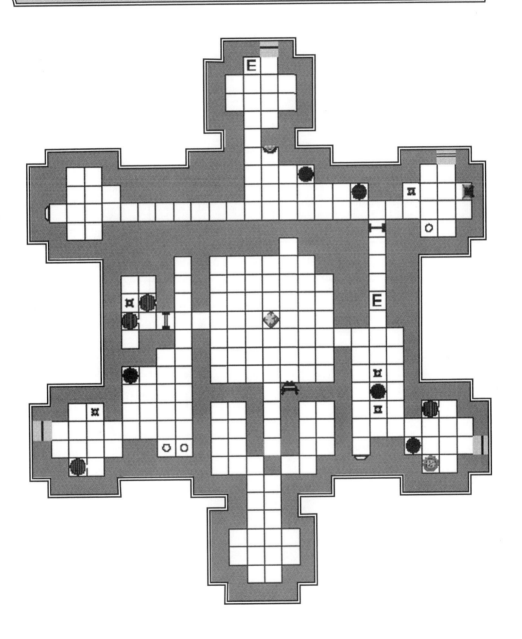

Level 1

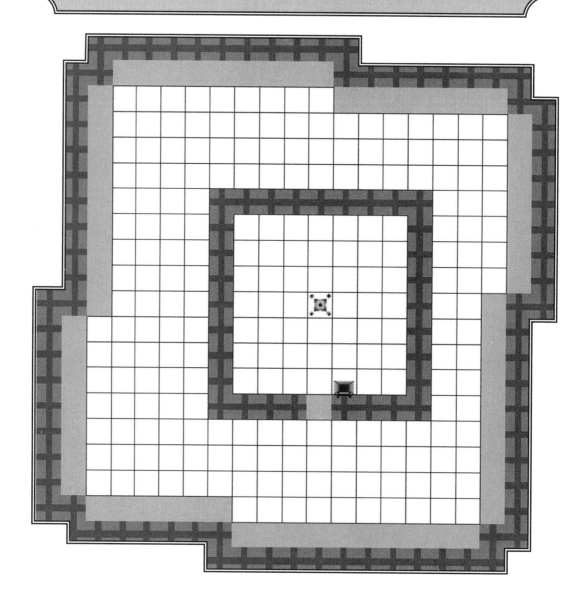

Individual Maps with Legends

These maps show each area you will travel though on your adventures, circled X's are pits.

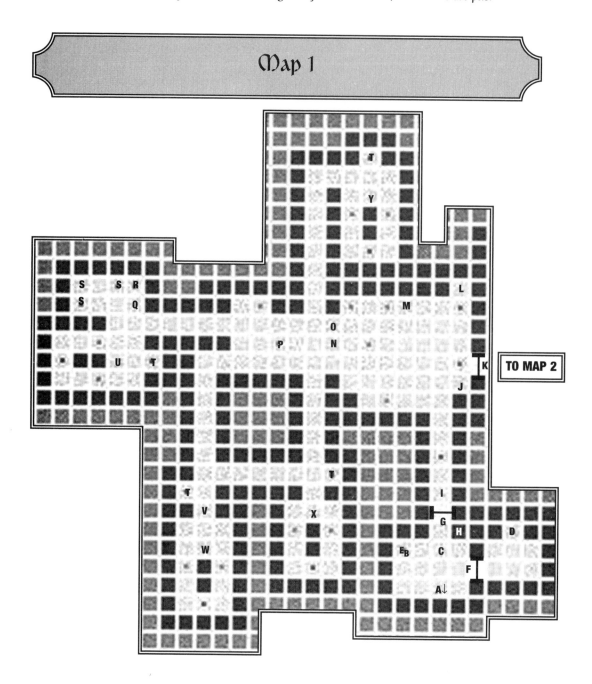

Map 1

TO MAP 2

Map 1 Legend

A   **Ladder down facing north**

B   **Table with one gold and bota**

C   **Chest with two healing potions**

D   **Altar #1 for resurrection**

E   **Niche facing south covered by sun crest, contains magic map, bag with various food items, money box with two gold coins, six copper coins**

F   **Door, unlocked**

G   **Door requires Solid key**

H   **Keyhole facing west for Solid key**

I   **Second keyhole facing east for Solid key**

J   **Keyhole facing west for Sun key**

K   **Door requires Sun key**

L   **Scythe**

M   **Niche facing south with magic marker**

N   **Teleport pad**

O   **Staff**

P   **Fountain with one gold coin, two copper coins**

Q   **Fountain facing west**

R   **Table with Sun key, Stamina potion**

S   **Table**

T   **Shop guard**

U   **Food shop inventory window facing east**

V   **Niche with protection potion facing east**

W   **Clothing shop inventory window facing north**

X   **Armor shop inventory window facing north**

Y   **Weapon shop inventory window facing north**

Map 2

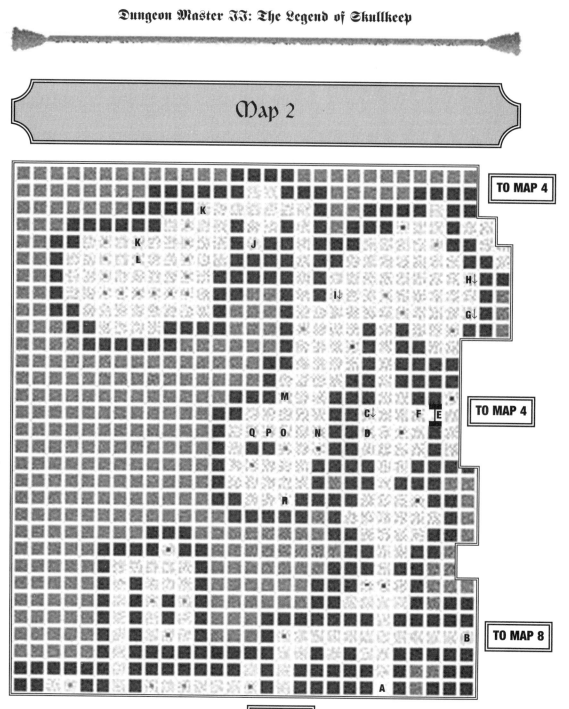

TO MAP 4

TO MAP 4

TO MAP 8

TO MAP 1

Map 2 Legend

LEVEL 6

A Locked door opened from Map 6

B Entrance to castle

C Ladder down facing east

D Dead bat

E Locked door requires Lightning key

F Keyhole facing south for Lightning key

G Ladder down facing north

H Ladder down facing south

I Ladder down facing east

J Mana blossom facing north

K Mana blossom facing south

L Altar #2 with Lightning key, magick map #2, bag with fire bomb, clan key piece #1

M Bow

N Quiver full of normal arrows

O Arrow

P Steak

R Thorn Demon regeneration point

Map 3

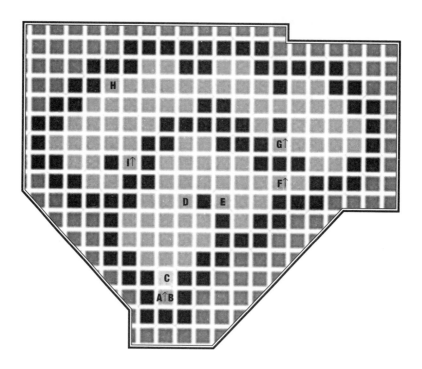

Map 3 Legend

LEVEL 7

A Ladder up facing east

B Niche facing west with two potions of cure poison

C Door unlocked

D Fountain facing west

E Strange gear device

F Ladder up facing north

G Ladder up facing south

H Green gem regeneration area facing south

I Ladder up facing east

Map 4

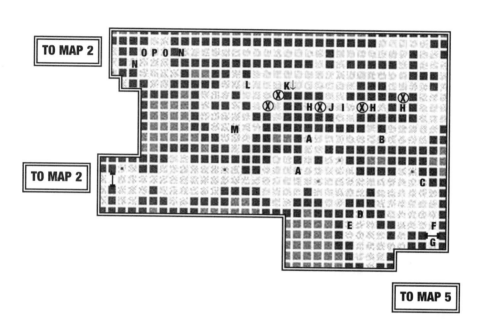

TO MAP 2

TO MAP 2

TO MAP 5

Map 4A

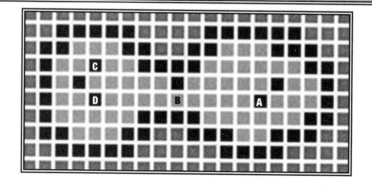

Map 4 Legend

LEVEL 6

A Fairy cushion regeneration point facing south

B Bainbloom regeneration point facing south

C Teleport pad and tech shield

D Steak

E Dump site for thief

F Keyhole facing west for Moon key

G Locked door requires Moon key

H Two gold coins, unreachable

I Skeleton, horned helm, chest with two gold, suzerain, and scarab

J Money box with one gold coin, one copper coin

K Ladder down facing north

L Niche facing south with bone

M Altar #3 with scout map, Moon key, clan key piece #2

N Wall disappears when approached from east

O Steak

P Crossbow, slayer arrow

Map 4A Legend

A Niche facing west with three potions of strength

B Huge boulder

C Ladder up facing north

D Niche facing north with three potions of strength

Map 5

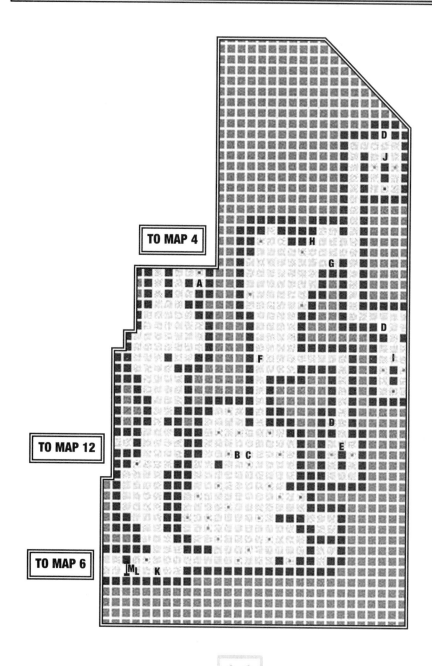

TO MAP 4

TO MAP 12

TO MAP 6

Map 5 Legend

LEVEL 6

A **Thief dump site, light/dark shield**

B **Invisible trigger, releases more axemen**

C **Altar #4 with Energy key, Clan key piece #3**

D **Shop guard**

E **Armor shop window facing north**

F **Palmapple regeneration point facing east**

G **Palmapple regeneration point facing west**

H **Palmapple regeneration point facing south**

I **Clothing shop window facing north**

J **Weapon shop window facing north K Teleport pad**

L **Keyhole facing north for Energy key**

M **Locked door requires Energy key**

Map 6

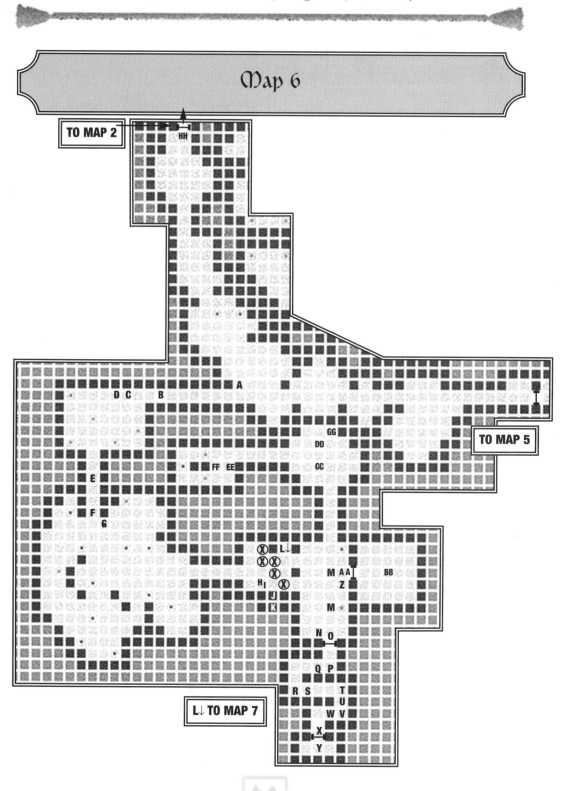

TO MAP 2

TO MAP 5

L↓ TO MAP 7

Map 6 Legend

Level 6

A Niche facing east with vorpal blade

B One-way door, allows passage to the west then closes

C Serpent staff

D Big crypt statue

E Fire bomb

F Spirit cap regeneration point facing east

G Palmapple regeneration point facing south

H Small boulder

I Niche facing north with button

J Wall disappears when button pressed

K Niche facing north with magickal box, Fire key

L Stairway down facing south

M Pillar

N Keyhole facing north for Fire key

O Locked door requires Fire key

P Mummy tomb 1 facing west

Q Floor trigger for tomb 1

R Tomb 2 facing east

S Floor trigger for tomb

T Tomb 3 facing south

U Floor trigger for tomb

V Tomb 4 facing north

W Floor trigger for tomb 4

X Unlocked door

Y Niche facing north, hidden behind tapestry, with two gold coins, fury, guard minion, Air key

Z Keyhole facing west for Air Key

AA Locked door requires Air key

BB Bartering table with Clan key piece #4

CC Blood fountain with fire bomb, one gold coin

DD Blood fountain with one gold coin

EE Tall brazier, no guard

FF Magick shop window facing east

GG Wall disappears when approached from south

HH Door opens when approached from south

Map 7

A↑ TO MAP 6

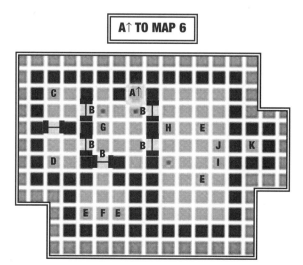

Map 7 Legend

LEVEL 7

A Stairway up facing south

B Randomly opening gates

C Foot plate

D Leg plate

E Pillar

F Niche facing north with mana potion

G Torso plate

H Armet

I Button facing west hidden behind small boulder

J Wall disappears when button pressed

K Chest with three red gems, one green gem, scarab

Map 8

S↑ TO MAP 9

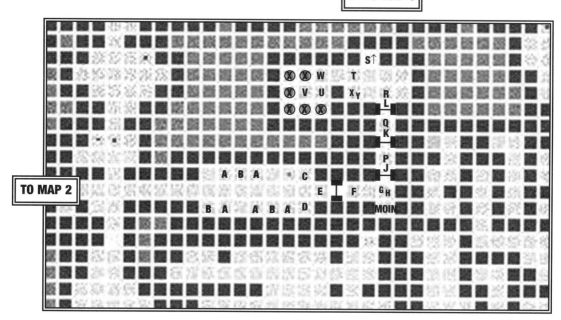

TO MAP 2

Map 8 Legend

A   Pillar

B   Tall brazier

C   Niche facing west with scroll, keyhole for Clan key pieces facing south

D   Niche facing west empty

E   Locked door requires all four Clan key pieces

F   Keyhole for Gold key, needed to go back out Clan key door

G   Skeleton, floor trigger closes all gates and releases two fireballs from the north (once)

H   Tech eye facing west

I   Floor trigger closes all gates (unlimited)

J   Gate 1

K   Gate 2

L   Gate 3

M   Wall trigger facing east, opens gate 1

N   Wall trigger facing west, opens gate 2

O   Wall trigger facing north, opens gate 3

P   Floor trigger, opens gate 1

Q   Floor trigger, opens gate 2

R   Floor trigger, opens gate 3

S   Stairs up facing south

T   Niche facing south with Gold key, minion map

U   Ladder down facing west, to small room with 2 fire bombs

V   Tempest

W   Invisible floor trigger opens pit at one square east if tempest is taken

X   False wall

Y   Niche facing north with crystal shield

Map 9

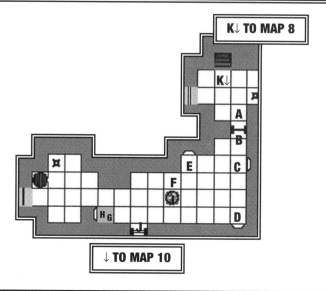

K↓ TO MAP 8

↓ TO MAP 10

Map 9 Legend

LEVEL 5

A Bell rope facing west summons Vexirk to open gate from inside

B Locked gate opened by Vexirk

C Niche facing west with Mana blossom, spirit cap

D Niche facing north with meteor metal, staff

E Niche facing south with scroll, one gold coin

F Niche facing south with red gem

G False wall

H Niche facing east with combat staff

I Vexirk cauldron

J Locked door opened with numen staff

K Stairs down to Map 8

Map 10

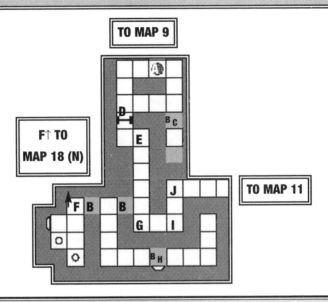

TO MAP 9

F↑ TO MAP 18 (N)

TO MAP 11

Map 10 Legend

A Floor trigger opens door at D (temporarily)

B False wall

C Button facing west opens wall

D Door opened with floor trigger

E Tech eye facing west, cover plate facing east covers removable tech eye

F Raised ladder up in ceiling unclimbable until later

G Tech eye facing north, cover plate facing south

H Niche facing north with light/dark helm

I Tech eye facing west, cover plate facing east

J Tech eye facing south, cover plate facing north

Map 11

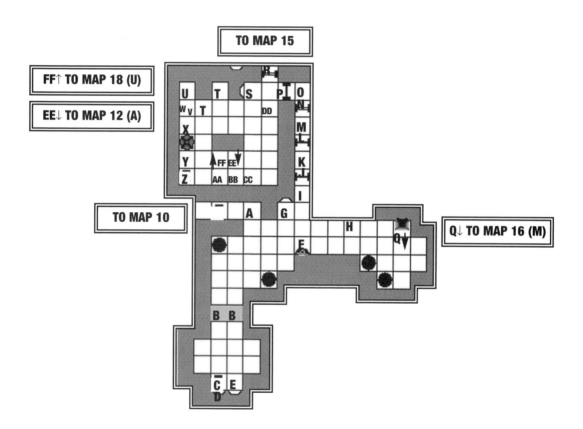

TO MAP 15

FF↑ TO MAP 18 (U)

EE↓ TO MAP 12 (A)

TO MAP 10

Q↓ TO MAP 16 (M)

Map 11 Legend

LEVEL 5

A Fireball ports facing west

B False wall

C Teleport pad

D Niche facing north with light/dark plate

E Niche facing north with light/dark polyen

F Fountain facing north

G Niche facing south with large gear, eye of time

H Locked door opened from north

I Keyhole facing west for large gear opens door 1

J Door 1 requires large gear

K Keyhole facing west opens door 2

L Door 2

M Keyhole facing west opens door 3

N Door 3

O Keyhole facing south opens door 4

P Door 4

Q Ladder down facing south

R Locked door requires trigger at T

S Niche facing east with earth key, blue minion portal facing south

T Keyhole facing east for Earth key, trigger facing south unlocks door

U Large gear

V Enemy guard minion spot

W Lever facing east turns on boiler

X Boiler

Y Sign 1 facing east

Z Teleport pad

AA Water gauge facing north

BB Fire gauge facing north

CC Sign 2 facing north

DD Blue minion portal facing west

EE Ladder down facing south, lever facing east lowers ladder

FF Raised ladder up facing south, unclimbable until later

Map 12

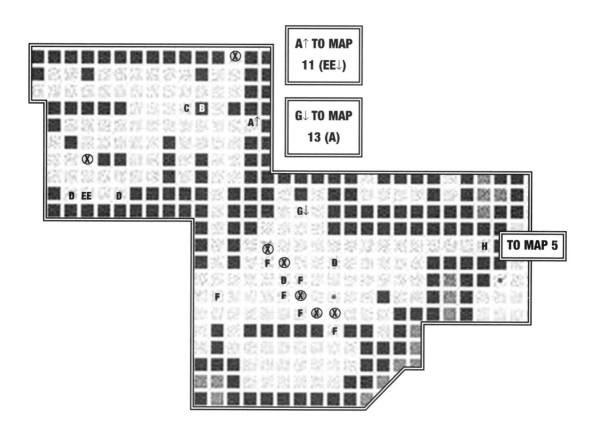

A↑ TO MAP
11 (EE↓)

G↓ TO MAP
13 (A)

TO MAP 5

Map 12 Legend

LEVEL 6

A Ladder up facing south

B Furnace facing west

C Enemy guard minion spot

D Stone pillar

E Pyro mine cart facing north, empty

F Huge boulders

G Ladder down facing south, one-way

H Wall disappears when approached from west

EE Teleport location from Map 13

Map 13

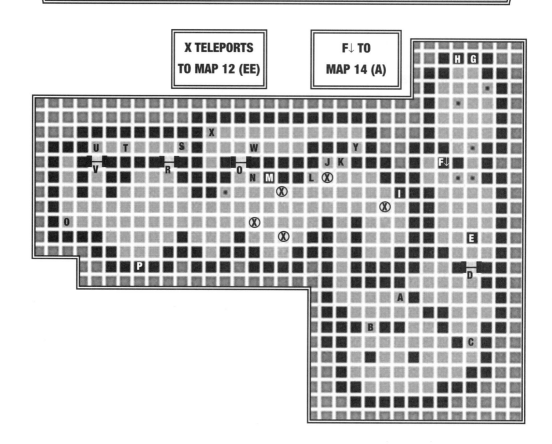

X TELEPORTS
TO MAP 12 (EE)

F↓ TO
MAP 14 (A)

Map 13 Legend

LEVEL 7

A Ladder up facing south, cut off and unclimbable

B Huge boulder

C Invisible floor trigger releases three skeletons

D Gate unlocke

E Green gem regeneration point facing south

F Ladder down facing west

G Niche facing south with kalan gauntlet

H Green gem regeneration point facing south

I Green gem regeneration point facing west

J Green gem regeneration point facing east

K Earth key after dropped from boiler room

L Green gem regeneration point facing east

M Niche facing south with emerald orb

N Keyhole facing south for blood key

O Locked gate requires blood key

P Green gem regeneration point facing north

Q Green gem regeneration point facing east

R Unlocked gate

S Spiked wall

T Floor trigger starts spiked wall moving west

U Trigger facing east opens gate at once

V Gate unlocked from south

W Trigger facing north activates teleport field

X Teleport field to Map 12, EE

Y Rockie regeneration area

Map 14

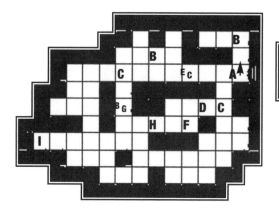

A↑ TO
MAP 13 (F)

Map 14 Legend

LEVEL 8

A Ladder up facing west

B Lava pit

C Lava pit releases lava monster if party moves within one space

D Blue gem facing north

E Blue gem facing south

F Skeleton with axe facing north

G Invisible floor trigger causes cave-in one space south

H Invisible floor trigger causes cave-in both here and at D

I One gold coin

Map 15

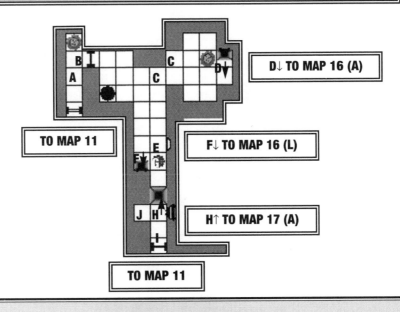

D↓ TO MAP 16 (A)

TO MAP 11

F↓ TO MAP 16 (L)

H↑ TO MAP 17 (A)

TO MAP 11

Map 15 Legend

LEVEL 5

A Keyhole 2 facing west for Earth key

B Locked door requires Earth key

C Blue portals facing south and east

D Ladder down facing south

E Niche facing west with scout map

F Ladder down facing north

G Floor trigger activates ZO balls

H Ladder up facing west

I Door opens from north

J Wall lever facing south deactivates ZO balls

Map 16

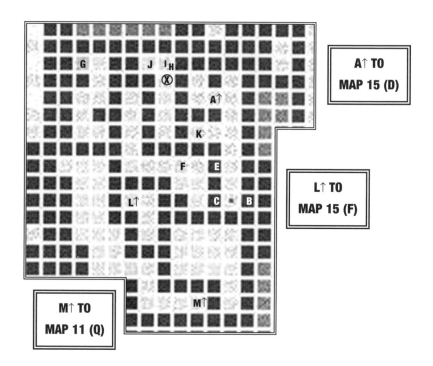

A↑ TO
MAP 15 (D)

L↑ TO
MAP 15 (F)

M↑ TO
MAP 11 (Q)

Map 16 Legend

LEVEL 6

A Ladder up facing south

B Wall button facing west, closes wall one space north and opens wall one space west

C Tech boots

D Wall button facing south, turns on reflector one space west and opens wall allowing passage to G

E Wall button facing west, releases fireballs

F Tech plate

G Teleporter field to A

H Tech polyen

I Wall button facing south opens pit one space south and turns on teleporter field one space west

J Teleporter field to D

K Wall button facing north, closes wall at one space south (toggle)

L Ladder up facing north

M Ladder up facing south

Map 17

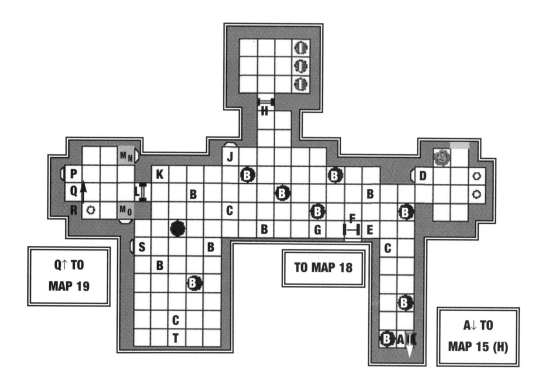

Q↑ TO
MAP 19

TO MAP 18

A↓ TO
MAP 15 (H)

Map 17 Legend

LEVEL 4

A Ladder down facing west

B Pillar

C Obstacle device

D Niche facing east with scroll

E Keyhole facing north for
Master key

F Locked door required large
gear and master key

G Keyhole facing north for
Large gear

H Unlocked door

I Floor trigger releases
Medium fireball

J Niche facing south with 8
slayer arrows

K Keyhole facing south for
vacuum fuse

L Locked door required vacuum
fuse

M False wall

N Niche facing west with
light/dark shield

O Niche facing north
with light/dark greave

P Niche facing east with
master key

Q Raised ladder up facing east,
requires cross key

R Keyhole facing north for cross
key

S Niche facing east with eight
slayer arrows

T Niche facing north with
large gear

Map 18

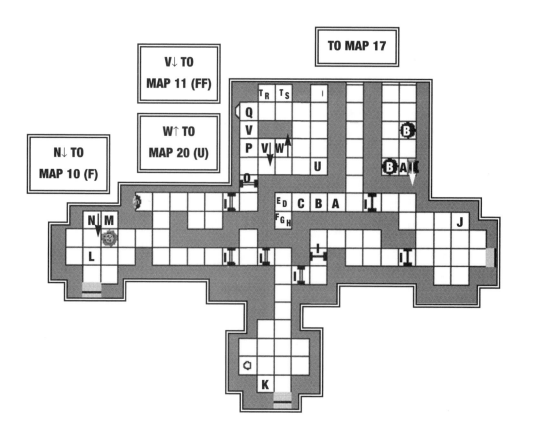

Map 18 Legend

LEVEL 4

A Scout map

B Wall lever facing south (all levers open doors in up position)

C Wall lever facing south

D Wall lever facing south

E Wall lever facing east

F Wall lever facing east

G Wall lever facing north

H Wall lever facing west

I Door opened by levers

J Barrel with kalan gauntlet

K Barrel with two fire bombs

L Barrel with vacuum fuse and two poison bombs

M Wall lever facing south, lowers ladder

N Ladder down facing south

N Ladder down facing south

O Locked door requires Master key, lock is on door

P Keyhole facing east for vacuum fuse

Q Niche facing east with Cross key

R Lever facing east operates pumps 1

S Lever facing west operates pumps 2

T Pumps facing south

U Blue minion portal

V Lever facing west, lowers ladder facing south

W Raised ladder facing south, unclimbable until later

Map 19

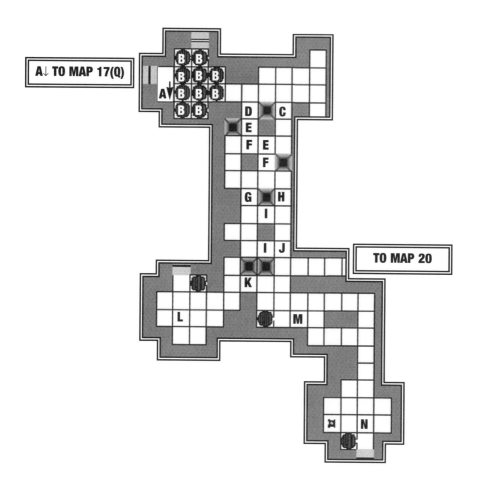

A↓ TO MAP 17(Q)

TO MAP 20

Map 19 Legend

LEVEL 3

A Ladder down facing east

B Table

C Ram facing west

D Ram facing east

E Ram facing west, another facing south

F Ram facing north, another facing east

G Ram facing east

H Ram facing west

I Ram facing north, another facing south

J Ram facing west

K Ram facing north

L Table with two guard minions

M Table with attack minion

N Table with guard minion

Map 20

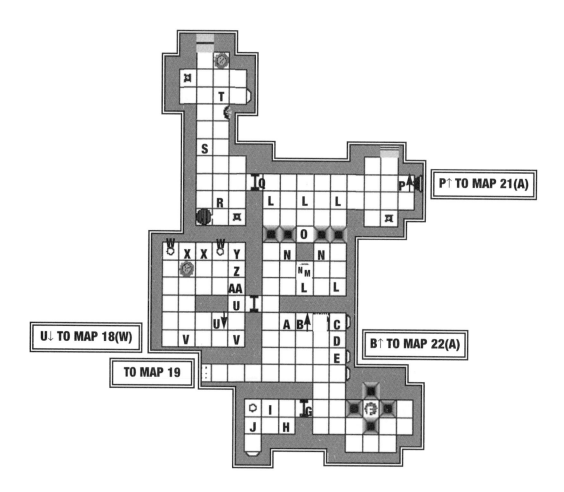

P↑ TO MAP 21(A)

U↓ TO MAP 18(W)

B↑ TO MAP 22(A)

TO MAP 19

Map 20 Legend

LEVEL 3

A Sign facing south

B Raised ladder facing south, unclimbable

C Niche facing west with empty flask

D Nich facing west with poison bomb

E Niche facing west with fire bomb

F Floor trigger, object sensitive, removes pits and opens door at G

G Locked door requires floor trigger

H Fury

I Fire polyen

J Male fire plate

K Locked door requires Master key, lock on door

L Reflector

M Floor trigger releases fireball

N Levers facing west, south, east all move reflectors, fireball port facing north

O Target symbol on floor

P Ladder up facing west

Q Locked gate requires fireballs to force open

R Fire helm

S Fire greave

T Fire shield

U Lever facing east, lowers ladder facing south

V Fire valve facing north

W Pipe obstacle

X Water valve facing south

Y Sign facing south

Z Billows gauge facing west

AA Blue minon portal facing west

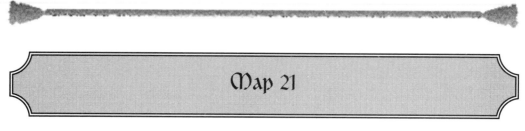

Map 21

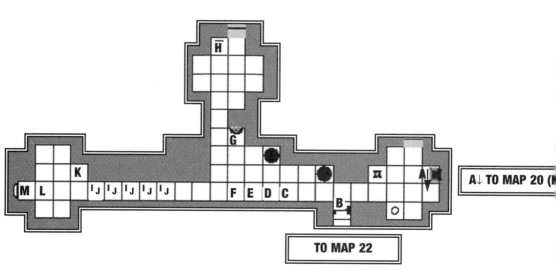

A↓ TO MAP 20 (

TO MAP 22

Map 21 Legend

LEVEL 2

A Ladder down facing west

B Locked door requires onyx key, lock on door

C Water gauge facing north

D Furnace gauge facing north

E Boiler gauge facing north

F Pumps gauge facing north

G Fountain facing south

H Teleport pad

I Lightining rod facing south

J Lightining rod facing north

K Knife switch facing west, turns off ligtning

L Suction trap on floor

M Niche facing east with onyx key and skull key, when both are removed, a suction trap is activated

Map 22

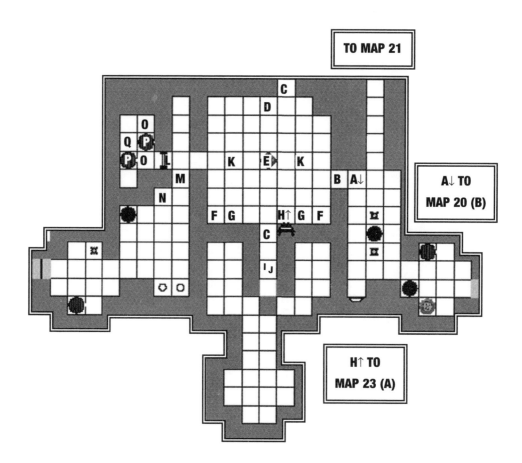

TO MAP 21

A↓ TO
MAP 20 (B)

H↑ TO
MAP 23 (A)

Map 22 Legend

LEVEL 2

A Raised ladder down facing south, requires lever

B Lever facing south lowers ladder

C Knife switch facing west activates lightning

D Lightning rod facing south

E Crystal device

F Knife switch facing north activates fireballs

G Fireball port facing north

H Ladder up facing north, knife switch facing west activates power for portal

I Attack minion

J Dimensional portal facing north

K Floor grate, also reflector position later

L Locked gate, opened from west

M Keyhole facing east for Skull key, activates teleport field

N Teleport field to one space north of Q

O Reflector

P Table

Q Tall brazier

Map 23

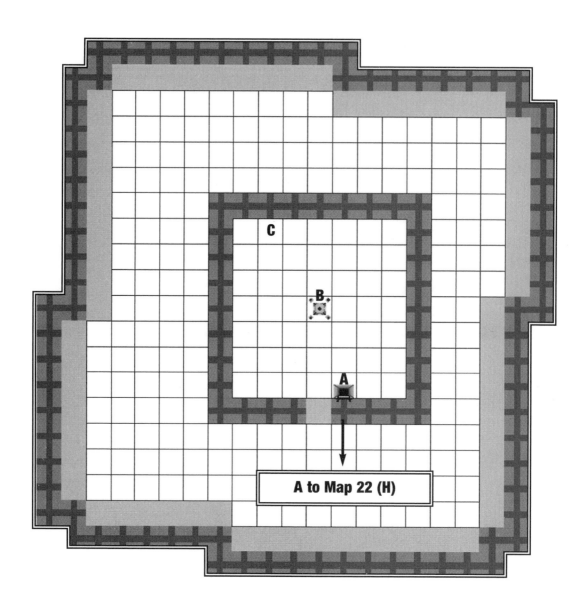

A to Map 22 (H)

Map 23 Legend

LEVEL 1

A   **Ladder down facing north**

B   **Storm lightning rod device**

C   **Blue medusa portal
    facing south**

Shop Prices

The following lists show the prices of items available in the various shops of the realm. The home village shops are located on Map 1. The other shops are located on Map 5, and the Magick Shop is on Map 6.

The following is a list of all the items to be found in the shops, as well as their prices. The wholesale (W) price is the price that the shop will buy the item at. The retail price (R) is what the shop will sell for.

Armor

Item	Home Village		Other Village		Magic Shop	
	R	W	R	W	R	W
Quiver	5	6	5			
Horned Helm	28	24	24	20		
Mail Helm		36	30	45	38	
Helm		66	54	66	54	
Bascinet	96	80	114	93		
Great Helm	180	152	153	120		
Armet	216	180	216	180		
RA SAR Helm	396	324				
Fire Helm		32	360			
Tech Helm	57	45	519	420		
Breast Plate	136	112	108	90		
Torso Plate	290	228	290	228		
Mirthal Plate	387	312	387	312		
RA SAR Plate			201	165		
Fire Plate (M)	708	584	584			
Fire Plate (F)	720	612	612			
Tech Plate	204	168	372	309		
Thigh Plates	66	54	52	44		
Leg Plate	137	113	137	113		
Mithral Huke	285	228	285	228		
RA SAR Poleyn	528	432				
Fire Poleyn	549	450				
Tech Poleyn	70	57	528	432		
Greaves	39	33	49	41		
Foot Plate	92	76	92	76		
RA SAR Greave		264	216			
Fire Greave	290	228	198			
Tech Boots	396	324	264	216		
Wood Shield	8	8	11	9		
Small Shield	48	40		48	40	
Crystal Shield		180	180	164		
SAR Shield	216	180				
RA SAR Shield	396	324				
Tech Shield	456	372	305	240		
Fire Shield	432	360				

Weapons

Item	Home Village R.	Home Village W.	Other Village R.	Other Village W.	Magic Shop R.	Magic Shop W.
Torch	1	1	2	2	2	2
Dagger	12	8	2	2		
Scythe	24	16	18			
Machete	24	16	44	36		
Sword	86	57	78	65		
Rapier	120	80	90			
Axe	144	96		26	22	
Sabre	192	128	144			
Katana		164	224	180		
Excsymyr	420	280	312			
Blue Steele	600	400	85			
Vorax	168		720	594		
Vorpal Blade	420	372				
Tempest	672	912	780	720	672	
ZO Blade	804	912	852			
Fury	960	1332	1098	360	327	
Club		4	4	4	4	
War Club	8	6	16	14		
Mace	48	66	54			
Morningstar	112	153	120			
Tech Mace	450	300	480			
Sling	6	4	1	1		
Quiver	6	4	5			
Bow		24	16	4	4	
Crossbow	120	84	88	72		
Speedbow	198	162				
Arrow	1	1	3	3		
Slayer Arrow	6	6	6			
Poison Dart	6	4	5	5		
Shuriken	8	6	7	7		
Staff	8	6	7	7		
Rainbow Wand	93	85				
Rogue Staff	112	130	117			
Bainbloom	64	72	84	76		
Large Gear	17	15				
Vacuum Fuse	385	312				
Spiral Staff	201	180				
Staff of NETA	161	147				
Emerald Orb	396	360				
Serpent Staff	530	480				
Combat Staff	480	432				
Strom Ring	960	864				
Kalan Gauntlet	1920	1665	208	180		
Attack Minion	240	228				
Guard Minion	210	180				

Clothing and Necklaces

Item	Home Village R.	W.	Other Village R.	W.	Magic Shop R.	W.
Cape	6	6	4	4		
Cloak of Night	27	23	33	27	21	19
Bandanna	1	1	1	1		
Black Top	13	11	13	11		
Tunic	17	15	17	15		
Fine Robe Top	26	22	22	18		
Bodice	26	22	26	22		
Doublet	33	27	33	27		
Leather Jerkin		60	51	51	42	
Brigandine	83	69	83	69		
Scale Hauberk	176	144	210	168		
Tabard	8	8	8	8		
Black Shirt	13	11	13	11		
Gunna	18	16	18	16		
Blue Pants	15	13	19	17		
Fine Robe	26	22	22	18		
Huke	30	26	30	26		
Leather Pants	45	38	38	32		
Scale Mail	105	87	105	87		
Sandals	3	3	2	2		
Leather Boots	15	13	13	11		
Black Boots	26	22		22	18	
Mithral Hosen	198	162		198	162	
Rune Charm	25		25		28	26
Jewel of Symal	49					
Illumulet	81	81				
Moonstone	117	117	136	120		
Mezmar	168	168	197	177		
Clan Chief Gem	240	240	281	240		
Suzerain	372	372	432	396	480	432

Food and Supplies

Item	Home Village		Other Village		Magic Shop	
	R.	W.	R.	W.	R.	W.
Apple	1	1				
Jicama	3	3				
Worm Round	2	2				
Bread	3	3				
Cheese	4	4				
Shank	6	6				
Steak	13	11				
Palm Apple	13	11	12	12		
Mana Blossom	54	45	52	48		
Fairy Cushion	88	72	84	76		
Spirit Cap	132	108	120	114		
Flask	17	15				
Compass	11	9				
Bota		2	2			
Water Flask	16	16				
Health Potion	25	23				
Cure Poison	21	19				
Mana Potion	29	27				
Dexterity Potion	37	35				
Strength Potion		50	45			
Wisdom Potion	42	38				
Vitality Potion		45	42			
Poison Bomb	168	152				
Fire Bomb	228	209				

Nuts and Bolts

Ah, now it is time to tell you the nuts and bolts of our adventuring, in hopes that you may learn from it.

You must understand that everything is referenced in a number of ways. We have, first, the problem of how to break things down. The best manner of dealing with this is to follow Tanic's idiotic quest idea. You cannot escape each area until certain jobs are accomplished, finding of keys, solving of puzzles, that sort of thing. Hence, we will treat each of these jobs as a quest.

Next, there are many references to the maps I drew on my travels. Since there are several maps, I have referenced them numerically. Looking at the maps in the previous chapter, you'll see that each one is numbered and letters are used to mark items and points of interest on the maps. When I am talking about a specific spot, I will give the map number and the letter. For instance 1A, would be map one, location A, which happens to be the ladder down to the Hall of Champions in Quest 1.

You see, it is all really quite simple. That is not to say thinking these things out isn't thirsty work. Barkeep!

Overviews

THESE ARE THE OVERVIEWS OF THE QUESTS.
DON'T WORRY ABOUT MEMORIZING THEM RIGHT NOW; THEY WILL BE REPEATED
AS WE TALK ABOUT THE PARTICULAR QUESTS. BUT THIS WILL HELP GIVE
YOU AN IDEA OF WHAT TO DO IN EACH QUEST.

Outdoors

Quest 1: Find Sun key, visit shops, open the Sun key door to escape area 1.

Quest 2: Acquire all items from the Lightning altar, defeat various nasties for food, open the Lightning door to escape area 2.

Quest 3: Get the fairy cushions, get the tech shield to teleport, avoid the wolves, acquire all items from the area, open the Moon door to escape area 3.

Quest 4: Defeat the thieves and axemen, visit three new shops, acquire keys from the Energy altar, open Energy door to escape area 4.

Quest 5: Temple quest: navigate through the cemetery and tree gorgon areas, visit the magick shop, acquire necessary keys, avoid moving pit traps, defeat the mummies and spectres, acquire armor and gems, get the last clan key piece.

Quest 6: Enter the castle, solve a gate puzzle, use the minion map, defeat the Numen, play with the cauldron, use the minion map again, remove the tech eyes, gather items, solve a door puzzle to reach the boiler room.

Quest 7: Descend to the castle catacombs, defeat various nasties, retrieve the Earth key, save the rockies, get lots of gems and weapons, return to the boiler room.

Quest 8: Optionally navigate the imp maze for armor, disarm the pit trap, deal with archer guards, get lots of slayer arrows, acquire the master key, solve a locked door maze to reach the pump room.

Quest 9: Use the cross key to go up, blow up tables, negotiate a maze with rams that push you into pits, reach the valve room, solve the reflector puzzle, acquire lots of items for the last battle.

Quest 10: Solve a key puzzle, get reflectors from a store room, position the reflectors, activate the devices (which may require a trip back to the catacombs), enter the dimensional portal.

Quest Breakdowns

Now I will try to tell you how to accomplish your goals.

Quest 2

Well, with some steaks in our belly and our combat system seeming to work pretty well, there wasn't any real way to avoid getting on with adventuring in earnest.

So off we went into the wilds of what was, we had agreed, the second quest. Almost all of the creatures we needed to worry about were killed in our former attacks. The only remaining creatures were the thorn demons, which seemed to multiply more quickly than we could hope to eat them. However, they pretty much stayed in the glen to the north and left us alone to poke about, experiment, and write things like "Tanic was here" on the walls of the castle.

Moving north, we came across a door. A slashed keyhole sat off to the side.

Tanic pushed on the door, but it stood fast.

"Locked," he said looking at me.

I looked back.

"Well, you're the wizard," he said.

I sniffed.

"We've had this discussion about doors before," I replied.

He smirked.

"You can't open doors can you?"

I knitted my brows together imperiously.

"Are you insinuating that with my great powers I can't open a mere door, if it wasn't for the fact that I felt doing so was beneath me?"

His smirk widened.

"Yeah, that pretty much sums it up."

We stared at each other for long minute.

"Well?"

"Well what?" I responded.

"Can you or can't you?"

"What?"

"Open the door."

"Well, er, not precisely, no."

Ravenblood snorted.

"Great, the wizard can't open the door. This is prime."

"So how are we going to get past it?" Tanic asked.

"Dunno, must be a key somewhere," said Ravenblood.

"That's it," said Tanic. "Just a matter of finding it."

And off we went.

Near the door there was a ladder down that looked promising. However, we didn't find a key in the hole at the bottom of the ladder. But there were a couple of cure poison potions, and a great gate.

On the other side of the gate were a number of bats.

"I hate bats," I said.

"Well, then, I guess we'll leave the gate closed for the moment, now won't we!" Tanic said.

"Nice place to rest, though," Ravenblood added.

But there was no key, so back up the ladder we went. Within a few minutes, we had explored the whole area from the edge of the thorn demon field, to the north, all the way down to a mysterious door to the south that refused to open and had no keyhole.

Don't think I didn't get a few more great wizard jokes at that point.

Finally it became obvious that the key to the first door was going to be either beyond the thorn demon glade or with the bats. There were some other ladders going down, but by pacing it off, we figured out that they must descend into the underground bat area.

"Bats or thorn demons?" asked Tanic.

"Bats," Zilch replied.

"Bats," said Ravenblood.

"Thorn demons?" I whined.

"Bats it is," said Tanic, heading down the nearest ladder, which was north of the safe ladder we had found earlier.

"I hate bats," I muttered as we descended into the darkness.

The bats attacked with a fury, but we cast spells on them and Zilch began his normal monster bashing.

In the distance, from the dim lights given off by our magickal illuminations, Tanic thought he saw something.

"West, double time."

We sprinted through the bats and found ourselves practically stumbling over a green gem embedded in the wall. I made a lunge for it, but Tanic was a hair quicker. There was brief struggle. He ended up with gem.

In the scuffle, one of the bats nipped Tanic, before Zilch smashed the bat with his ham-like fist.

We made it back up the ladder without anyone taking any more damage.

"Well that's not it. I think I feel a bit — " Tanic sat down on the ground abruptly.

Ravenblood ran up to him and rolled back an eyelid.

"Poison. Must be the bats."

Ravenblood took out one of the vials we had found in the caverns and poured it down Tanic's throat. He came around rapidly.

"Thank you, Ravenblood. I thought that might be the death of me."

Ravenblood just looked at him.

"The hypochondria of you, more likely. You should be able to keep going about forever through bat poison. I just gave you the cure to get the extra flask."

He turned and walked away.

It became obvious that the key, if key there was, was going to be in the glade with the thorn demons.

"Great. We had enough trouble killing them before, and it seems like there are more where those came from," I lamented.

"Avoid," said Zilch.

I started watching the thorn demons more closely. They did seem slow. It might be possible to run around them.

"Good plan. Lets just zip around them and take a little look see, shall we?"

Tanic took off at a run and the rest of us followed. It turned out to be pretty simple. I got bitten on the shoulder, but the damage was minor. We just stayed to the outside of the demons' area and made it all the way around.

At the top of the glade we found an altar. On the altar was another Magickal Map, the one that showed the magickal enhancements. There were also some mana blossoms, and not one, but two keys. We ran back out.

"Well, now we have two keys, eh," said Tanic. "Is that a bargain or what? I looked closely at the two keys.

"No, we have one key and one piece of a key. A clan key, unless I miss my bet, and a complete lightning key."

Tanic looked at the two and shrugged.

"Will it get us through the door?"

"Yea, the lightning key looks like it will fit."

"Well, then, let's get on with it."

We went to the second door and checked the key in the lock. It worked. A small cheer went up. We had completed the second quest, and — silly motivational tool that it was — the whole "quest" business did make us feel like this part of the trip was an accomplishment.

Tanic started to stride through the door.

"Er, don't you think we ought to wait?" I asked.

He looked at me menacingly.

"I agree," said Ravenblood. "We need to rest and practice a bit. Look, the ladder is right here, what say we nip down there and rest some. Looks secure enough for me."

Tanic weighed it and finally nodded his head and climbed down the ladder.

QUEST 2

Objectives: Acquire all items from the Lightning altar, defeat various nasties for food, open the Lightning door to escape area 2.

SEE MAPS 2 AND 3 ON THE NEXT PAGE.

Once outside the shop area, you will encounter many more monsters to deal with. Fight or evade your way north until you see the Lightning door, then go down the ladder at 2C. Aside from the castle entrance, this is the safest place to sleep in this area, plus you will find a couple of cure poison potions here. Leave the gate closed to keep bats out. After healing up and maybe getting in some target practice on the gate, go back up the ladder and venture north again to the thorn demon area. For now, don't provoke the thorn demons. They might push you around some and take a swipe or two, but it's fairly safe to walk quickly around them and collect the numerous items lying around. Go down the ladder at 2I, run north to grab the green gem at 3H and go back out before anyone gets poisoned. Now move on to the altar area, avoid the whirlwind, and gather up the altar items and mana blossoms. Go back to the ladder at 2C to rest and practice underground, then climb up and unlock the Lightning door.

Note that the green gem regenerates, though at a very slow rate. When coming through the area to go back to the shops, stop and check whether this gem has returned.

Map 2

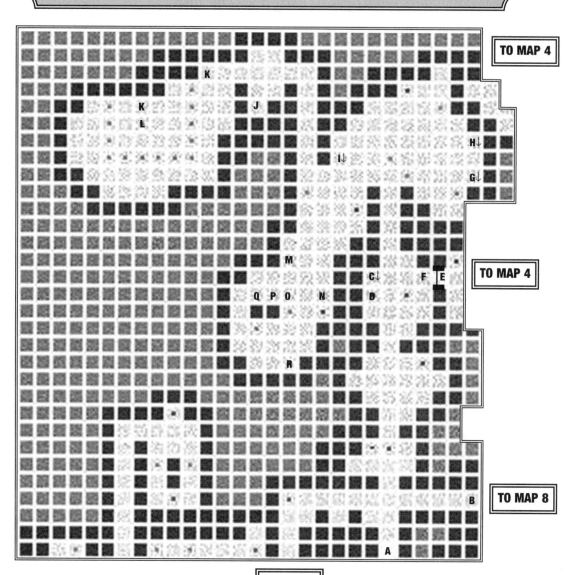

TO MAP 4

TO MAP 4

TO MAP 8

TO MAP 1

Map 3

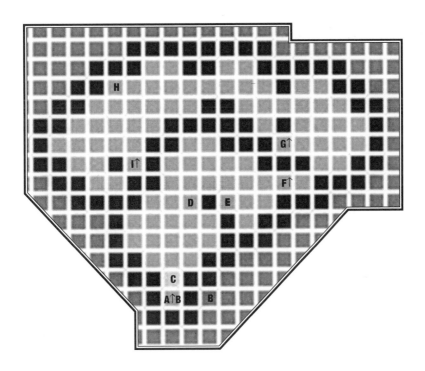

Quest 3

We trotted through the door, eyes and ears wide open for danger. This quest was likely to be more difficult than the last, mainly because I was running out of ale.

Right away a digger worm popped out of the ground only to meet the wrong end of Zilch's fist. Zilch was getting quite good at dispatching digger worms.

We found ourselves in a long, shrub-lined corridor. We walked a bit, and no one much noticed when Zilch dispatched another digger worm without effort.

However, Ravenblood was keeping his eyes open when, about halfway along the long shrub-line, it branched off.

"See that," he whispered to me.

I looked where he was clandestinely pointing.

"Yes, looks like a thorn demon pat to me."

"Worth a small mint."

"Thorn demon pats! I must have stepped in a ton of them back when we were at the Lightning altar. If only you had told me sooner — "

"No, you fraud. What is growing on it."

I looked closer.

"The mushroom!"

"That isn't just a mushroom. It's a fairy cushion. Worth about fifty coppers."

I looked at the thorn demon pat with more respect.

"Fifty coppers! Your sure!"

"Well, depends on the season and all, but that's about right."

We tried to look casual as we went over and inspected it more closely. Ravenblood picked it and put it in a small pouch on his belt.

"Hey, there's another one," I said.

I walked a bit to the east and picked the one I had spied. I put it in the pouch at my belt.

"What are you doing!" said Tanic, staring at me incredulously.

"Uh," I could see a good deal of ale money going for something silly, like supplies and armor. "Thorn demon dung. Important magickal component. A must-have for the spell of shill-shucking, you know."

He looked aghast.

"Thorn demon dung!"

I nodded solemnly.

"I guess that's why I will never make it far in magick. Give me good clean fighting blood any day."

"Well, different strokes, you know," I smiled.

He just shook his head, and right about then got blindsided by a four-foot man moving faster than it would seem possible.

The blow didn't appear to hurt him much.

Tanic spun.

"See here."

The little man was already practically across the clearing.

"Well, I have a mind to," he reached down to draw his sword, and his hand came back empty.

"The little bugger took my sword! Catch him!"

We ran after the dwarf, but he was much too fast for us. Finally he just disappeared around a bend at the end of the glade. We continued running, but came to an abrupt stop when Tanic fell head over heels.

"Arggh!"

He jumped up with a look of murder in his eyes, but then looked down at what had tripped him. His eyes narrowed and he picked up a shield that had been laying on the ground.

"Oh, nice!" He hefted the shield and swung it around a bit.

Then suddenly we were back at the village, standing amidst the shops.

I felt my stomach lurch.

"What the — !"

Ravenblood ran up and wrenched the shield off the still-stunned Tanic.

He examined it closely.

"Just as I thought. Tech shield. Don't go swinging this thing around."

Tanic protested.

"But I only — "

"You only pressed this button here," Ravenblood said. "Yeah, I know. This is a tech shield, oaf. Teleportation powers. Handy when you know what you are doing with them. Since you found it, I guess it is yours. But I would strongly advise you not to touch any of the buttons unless I tell you to."

> **THE TECH SHIELD WILL TELEPORT THE PARTY BETWEEN TELEPORTER PADS, LIKE THE ONE IT IS ORIGINALLY LOCATED BESIDE. ALL TELEPORTER PADS OUTSIDE YOUR HOME VILLAGE SEND YOU BACK HOME, AND USING THE ONE AT HOME SENDS YOU BACK OUT TO THE LAST ONE YOU USED.**

Tanic looked like he was about to reply in his own defense, but thought better of it before he opened his mouth, and just nodded instead.

The group went off to hit the shops, and I slipped away to the pub, where I got a bit more ale to fill my nearly empty pouch. And while I was there, it would have been a shame not to have a few for the road.

By the time I stumbled out of the pub I was more than a little happy. Then I saw him.

I pointed.

"You...you...thief!" I accused and hefted my staff into a striking position.

It was the fast dwarf from the thicket.

He just smiled, and, quicker than lightning, plucked the staff out of my hand. He cackled and ran off.

I started running after him, shouting.

Soon the rest of the party caught up with me. They must have heard my yells.

"What is your problem!" Tanic asked. He was looking spiffy, in a new breast plate.

Ravenblood crinkled up his nose.

"He's potted; that's what his problem is."

I shook my head vigorously, which had the interesting effect of unifying the two Ravenblood's I was seeing into a single one.

"Sober as a priest," I said.

"Well, there you go. He pleads guilty," said Tanic, laughing.

Ravenblood looked unamused.

"That little thief!" I said. "He's here."

Tanic looked at Ravenblood questioningly.

Ravenblood shrugged.

"Could be. Might have gotten caught in the edge effect of the tech shield."

Zilch growled and started running. We all followed his path with our eyes and saw the thief off in the distance, hiding behind a table.

We closed in on him, Ravenblood and I readying spells as we ran.

When we got close to him we yelled "duck" and fired, point blank.

Well, it was a long and arduous battle, since the little guy was so fast. But finally we killed him. My staff wasn't on him.

"Look around," said Ravenblood. "He has to have hidden his gains around here somewhere."

After searching for a bit, we finally found my staff.

"Ah, there we go," I said happily.

"I still don't have my sword back," Tanic muttered.

"Okay. Let's rest and then go back to the area we just came from and look for your sword," suggested Ravenblood.

Tanic sulked a bit. It was obvious he wanted to search for his sword right away.

"We have to get our spells back in order, Tanic. Be reasonable." I was seriously starting to wonder who was leading this party.

Tanic nodded his head, and we all set up camp and slept.

Well, maybe I did spend a few more minutes in the pub. But only a couple.

The next morning I had a terrible hangover, and the teleport back didn't help much at all.

After searching the area rather completely, we came up with Tanic's sword. He returned it to the sheath on his belt with a happy sigh.

Around the same area there was another locked door, which was not a surprise.

"Well, the only direction we haven't checked yet is that dogleg north of here going east. Let's go." Tanic said.

And off we went.

As we walked along the small pathway between the thickets, Ravenblood spotted another pair of fairy cushions that seemed to have sprung up in the same places as the set we took yesterday. He grabbed them both and put them in his pouch. A bit further on he pulled another plant I had never seen out of the ground.

"What's that?" I asked.

"Bainbloom," he replied. "Magickal in the extreme. Did you sleep though the mage's academy!"

Actually, Natural Herbs was an early morning class, and for various reasons that I don't need to go into now, I never tended to look and feel my best before noon.

I just scowled as we continued on.

By the time we caught up with the others, Zilch was climbing down his rope into a pit

"What's this!" asked Ravenblood.

"Well, we found this pit, and we are going to check to see what's in it," said Tanic.

Ravenblood and I followed Zilch down.

At the bottom, Zilch was moving a great boulder that blocked half the room.

Ravenblood looked down and saw a trio of vials on the ground. He picked one up and looked at it briefly.

"This is a strength potion. Zilch, this might help — "

Zilch gave a great grunt and the rock moved out of the way to uncover a corridor.

"Never mind," Ravenblood mumbled, putting the vials in his pack.

Tanic entered the hole at this point, yelling and sliding down the rope faster than I had ever seen anyone move except for free-falling.

"Wolves!" he exclaimed.

Ravenblood looked at him mildly.

"Big fighter like you can't kill a couple of dogs!"

"Shows how much you know, Mr. Smart Priest. Wolves run in packs. You swing on one and he howls. Well, then you are fighting a dozen of them. No, much better to just stay out of their way."

Ravenblood just shrugged.

Zilch was heading down the corridor he had uncovered, and we all followed him.

At the end of the corridor, there was a room with more potion and a ladder up.

Ravenblood examined the two potions.

"Strength," he said, handing them to me. I put them in my pack.

Zilch was starting up the ladder.

"Think we ought to rest here?" Ravenblood asked me.

I nodded my head yes and clipped Zilch behind the ear again with my staff. He fell unconscious to the ground. We undid his bedroll and put him on it. Then we all slept for a few hours, got up and horsed around a bit with spells and potions, slept some more, and finally climbed back out into the upper world.

The wolves were everywhere, but Ravenblood, with his keen eye, spotted a bone in a niche. He went out of his way to get it.

I got nipped by a wolf, and it took all of my self-control not to fry the beast.

"What are you doing playing with that bone?"

He just shook his head sadly at me and hurled the bone off into the distance.

I watched in amazement as the wolves all ran after it.

"Brilliant!" I said as I watched them go.

"Don't just stand there!" He barked. "They are going to bring it back."

We hustled around the next stand of trees and found an altar there. On it was the expected key, this one in the shape of a moon. There was also another Magickal Map and a piece of the partial key I was carrying. I fit the two together. We still needed at least one more piece.

We headed back east and found a poor soul who hadn't fared as well at the hands of the wolves. Among his remains, however, there were a number of items. We didn't take the time to look at them, as Ravenblood started to complain.

"My arm is getting tired from throwing this bone. We need to rest."

There was a nearby pit and we lowered ourselves into it to rest.

In the pit we went through the things we had found: a helm and some jewelry. I detected that the jewelry was magickal, so I took it. There was also some money, but I wasn't concerned with that when I felt the extra magickal power I was getting from the jewelry.

The next day, even though we had the key, we elected —actually Tanic elected—to continue searching the area, which proved fruitful. We found to the northeast some steaks and a crossbow with a fine arrow on it. Then we rested another night and, with more exhaustion than excitement, proceeded though the Moon door.

QUEST 3

Objectives: Collect the fairy cushions, get the tech shield to teleport, avoid the wolves, acquire all items from the area, open the Moon door to escape area 3.

See Maps 4 and 4A on page 203.

This area is best handled in three runs. The first run requires quickly running east to grab the two fairy cushions at the 4A locations then straight to the teleport pad at 4C where a tech shield lies on the pad. Nearby, a thief is prowling about and is likely to steal a couple of your items, so grab the shield and use it to teleport back to the shop area as quickly as possible. Unfortunately, doing so brings another thief into the shop area with you, but he won't enter the shops for fear of the guards. Sell the fairy cushions and any other unused items for cash, buy better equipment, and heal up. Go out and slay the thief since only one ever comes to this area, and remember that he puts items stolen in this area at 1L. This is good practice for dealing with monsters who take items. Also, Champions getting killed in the process is no problem here with the resurrection altar nearby. Once the area is secure, items are recovered, and the party is healed and prepared, begin the second run by teleporting back. Hopefully, the fairy cushions have regenerated (if the party has done some sleeping), so grab them, then move east into the wolves' area. Grab the bainbloom at 4B. As with the Thorn Demons, provoking the wolves is not recommended even though they tend to be more aggressive; attacking one outright causes them to howl and brings the entire pack to slay you, which they easily can do at this stage. Maneuver as quickly as possible to the first pit around the corner, face it without falling in, and use Graen's rope to descend safely down. Gather the strength potions in the niche. Drinking them is not necessary to move the boulder, just keep trying until it moves two spaces.

QUEST 3 (CONT.)

Grab more potions at the second niche and rest/practice as long as you like since there are no monsters to deal with here. Take the ladder up, and move quickly west to 4L, where you can grab the bone in the niche. This nifty item keeps the wolves busy. If you throw it, they'll go pick it up and bring it to you, attacking less often. As before, try not to provoke them even though you'll get bitten occasionally. Now go back east through the swamp to 4I where an unknown fallen warrior left some items to grab. Get them, and descend into a nearby pit to rest and distribute the goodies. The suzerain and scarab in the chest can both be worn in the pouch, giving the wearer a 15 point (total) mana boost.

Now for the last run: Go up the ladder and head west again, this time all the way around to the altar. The wolves should still try to bring the bone to you, so keep throwing it. Grab the stuff, go back to the ladder and rest if necessary, then leave the area by taking the corridor leading to 4N, where the wall of thickets will disappear and lead back to the thorn demon clearing, which now contains some new items. Head back to town to rest and barter with the shops, then teleport back and kill the thief who might or might not have regenerated. He hides his ill-gotten shinies at 4E. Recover stolen items and rest before opening the moon door.

Map 4

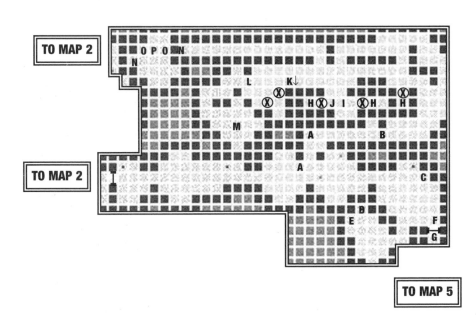

TO MAP 2

TO MAP 2

TO MAP 5

Map 4A

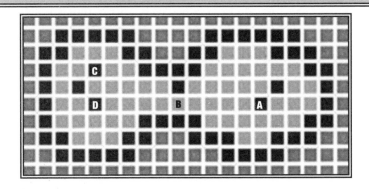

Quest 4

The next quest was actually quick work. On the other side of the door were some digger worms and a couple more of the thieves, but we dispatched all of them fairly easily, though we did stop to rest once.

To the north, we found the thieves' bolt hole. It held yet another nice shield, which Zilch took.

Then we went to the teleport pad and used the shield to run back to town and rest up a bit.

The one interesting thing we did run into, however, was the axemen.

"Look at that, now, will you!" said Tanic.

A group of humans were crossing the glade toward us.

I wondered if they might have a spot of ale on them.

This thought was cut short when they started hurling axes at us. Great sharp things, they were.

"Attack!" Tanic yelled and started to run forward. He was brought up short by Ravenblood grabbing the back of his cloak.

"You might want to think this out."

"They are attacking us!"

Ravenblood picked up an ax near his leg.

"These things are worth good money back in town. Let's just collect them and teleport back."

Tanic stood indecisive for an instant, but Ravenblood and I were collecting axes as quickly as we could.

Finally, Tanic gave up and started helping us.

Right before the axemen were upon us, we ran back to the teleport pad and returned to town.

Having sold the axes for a pretty penny in the shops, we went back to the glade three times, getting the fools to throw their money at us.

Finally, when they ran out of axes, we had to dispatch them. I think we were all rather sad about it until Tanic accidentally pressed a button near the altar and let out another flood of the creatures.

All was joy for a bit as we started our ax-trading ring again, but all good things must end. And this group of barbarians ran out of axes finally, but still tried to fight.

After polishing them off, we rested for a bit, ate heartily, and talked about trying to start a worldwide ax-trading empire.

It turns out the axemen had a small village, and we traded there for some items that were cheaper than those back home. And, finally, we proceeded through the door to our next quest.

Yes, it was a bright time for us, but things were not to be as easy after this.

QUEST 4

Objectives: Defeat the thieves and the axemen, visit three new shops, acquire keys from the Energy altar, open the Energy door to escape area 4.

SEE MAP 5 ON THE NEXT PAGE

Beyond the Moon door are the usual worms, as well as two more thieves to deal with. By now the party should have plenty of practice and little difficulty killing the thieves, so, since they follow you around more than other monsters, take them out to prevent future thefts. Their dump site at 5A has a nice shield in it, so grab it. This isolated area is also a good place to trap them in with Guard Minions, if the party's spell-casters are proficient with this highly useful spell. Proceed south to the teleport pad at 5K and port back to town to rest, then port back and enter the axeman area. At first, defeating the axemen isn't as important as collecting the axes they throw. Keep the scout map active, keep moving and picking up axes as you go, and recover the items they take from you at their dump site, which is one block north from the axeman trigger at 5B. Be careful not to get trapped by them because they might be too powerful for the party to handle. Set an occasional Guard Minion to weaken them and escape back to the teleport pad to sell the axes in town. Axes sell for 96 coppers at home, as opposed to 22 coppers at the weapon shop near the axemen. This is an excellent source of income for a party still lacking in quality wares, so make several trips. Once the axemen have been cheated out of their weapons, they're much easier to defeat individually with standard hit-and-run tactics. Remember that an invisible trigger on the west side of the altar releases more armed axemen, so wait until the ones already in the area are dead before adding to their numbers. Spend your hard-earned cash at the new shops, feast on palmapples, rest, and grab the keys from the altar at your leisure before moving on to the next quest. Don't forget to train.

Map 5

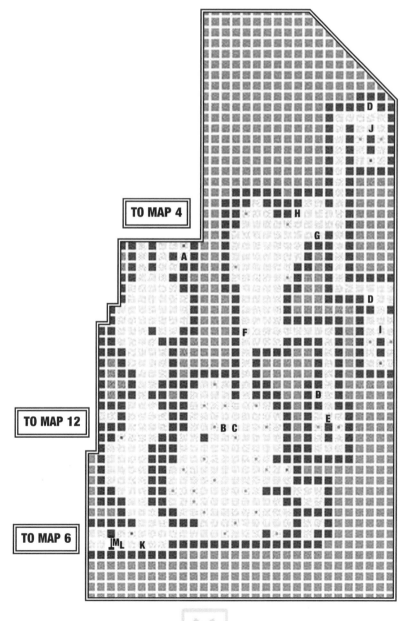

TO MAP 4

TO MAP 12

TO MAP 6

Quest 5

By the time we were on this quest, we had the whole process down to a rather boring routine. We ran in, kept jogging, and killed anything that got between us and the way out of the area. Not much of an effort really. The jogging was annoying, but we rested frequently and headed back into one of the two villages at the slightest excuse, so the ale bag didn't run dry.

We ran into the area and sprinted straight into a minion, but it took all of two minutes to dispatch the pesky bugger. Then we found a vorpal sword for our trouble. Zilch, who up to this point had shown no real interest in using weapons, decided the vorpal sword was his kind of weapon, and without comment slung it over his shoulder.

The next place we stumbled into was a cemetery with some crypts and a statue in the center.

I looked at one of the crypts and started toward it.

"Wouldn't do that if I were you," Ravenblood said.

"People get buried with all manner of treasure," I told him, trying to make up for my previous lack of botanical knowledge.

"Spirits don't like to be disturbed," he replied.

I put my hands on the lid of one of the crypts.

"You listen to too many wive's tales," I said as I heaved on the lid.

The spectre that emerged took what I felt was an entirely gratuitous swipe at me.

Being the brave hero that I am, I dove behind Tanic.

"Begone foul beaste," shouted Tanic as he drew his blade and...
did nothing.

Not, to give the fool credit, that he didn't try. However, his blade simply passed through the apparition. This sort of thing could give an adventuring type the willies.

I rolled left, pulled up my runes, and launched a fireball.

The spectre might have been amused, but it was hard to tell, seeing as how it was just a floating robe.

This was starting to look ugly.

Tanic took a robe to the head and stumbled back.

Then Zilch ran in from the side and cleaved the thing at just about the same time that Ravenblood fired off a spell. Between the two of them, they hurt the undead beastie pretty badly.

In a few moments, the two of them had finished it off, with Tanic and me just watching in amazement.

"How did you do that?" Tanic asked Zilch.

"Hit it," Zilch replied.

"Well, I hit it too."

"Must have hit it harder," said Zilch, and then he guffawed.

Tanic marched off to the south in a huff.

We followed, with Zilch looking at Tanic every once in a while and saying, "harder" and then laughing. Tanic ignored him and kept marching.

"So how did you do it?" I asked Ravenblood.

"Right spell," he said. "You need to use DES EW. Only that spell works properly against undead."

I pulled out the runes and made sure I had them ready, in case we ran against another one of the things.

"So what about Zilch? "

"That sword we found was a vorpal sword. The only weapon that hurts undead."

I was still mulling this over when we came to the tree. It was a great, gnarled thing.

We passed it and started trekking across a swamp, and at that point I happened to look over my shoulder.

The tree was following us.

At first, I tried to remember how much ale I had drunk that day. Then I looked back again.

The tree was definitely following us.

"Uh, Ravenblood. Take a look behind us and tell me if you see anything strange."

He looked over his shoulder and then stopped.

After looking at the tree for a moment, he started running away from it.

He rapidly outdistanced Zilch and Tanic.

"Run, you fools! Tree gorgon!" We all sprinted, finally stopping on the steps of a temple, totally winded.

"What," gasped out Tanic. "Is a tree gorgon?":

"Nasty business, that is what a tree gorgon is," Ravenblood said. "Does great amounts of damage with its branches. Not worth fighting if you can run away."

I, at least, felt that way about most everything we had met.

Inside the temple we grabbed everything that wasn't nailed down in the same heroic way that we stole everything we ran across.

Then it was back to the shops for another round of trading. We came back fully equipped the next day, iced another group of nasty undead, and negotiated a rather complex group of moving pits.

And then we found the key, but unfortunately it was guarded by a phantom shop keeper.

The ghost stood in front of his trading table. On his side of the table was the key we needed.

"So what do we do now?" Tanic asked.

"Take the key," I said. "You're the fighter."

Tanic made a lunge for the key and blew it.

So much for that idea.

I thought about it for a second.

"Trade with him."

I pulled out a gold coin and dropped it on the table. The phantom slid the key over.

The phantom let out a deep, haunting laugh as he faded out.

"What are you laughing at?" I snapped.

"I would have taken a copper."

Quest 5

Objectives: Navigate through the cemetery and tree gorgon areas, visit the magick shop, acquire necessary keys, avoid moving pit traps, defeat the mummies and spectres, acquire armor and gems, get the last clan key piece.

See Maps 6 and 7 on the next two pages

The focus of this quest is to recover the last clan key piece, but first you'll want to make a run to the magick shop. Keep on the lookout for any wandering monsters, then move directly west and grab the vorpal blade at 6A. Proceed into the cemetery and get the serpent staff, but be very careful not to walk directly in front of the nearby crypt with the statue at 6D, or the one in the center of the cemetery to the southwest of the statue. Doing so releases an angry spirit that is immune to most attacks, so tread carefully south and west to the next area. Pick up the fire bomb and the spirit cap on the way and save them to sell later.

From here, get through the haunted forest as fast as possible by running south until you meet an evil tree, then turn east and trudge directly through the swamp to reach the temple. These trees are tough and yield only a pile of wood once killed, so if you really need the fighting experience you can attack them, but it's not recommended due to the ugly damage they inflict. Once inside the temple, rest and get the hidden items revealed by pressing a switch at 6I. The covered pits on the southernmost side of the room are safe to tread on, so cross these, move to the northeast edge of the room you are now in, and stand here momentarily to activate the scout map. Monitor the mobile pits in the next room, and when it appears safe, move quickly across and north out of the temple.

Map 6

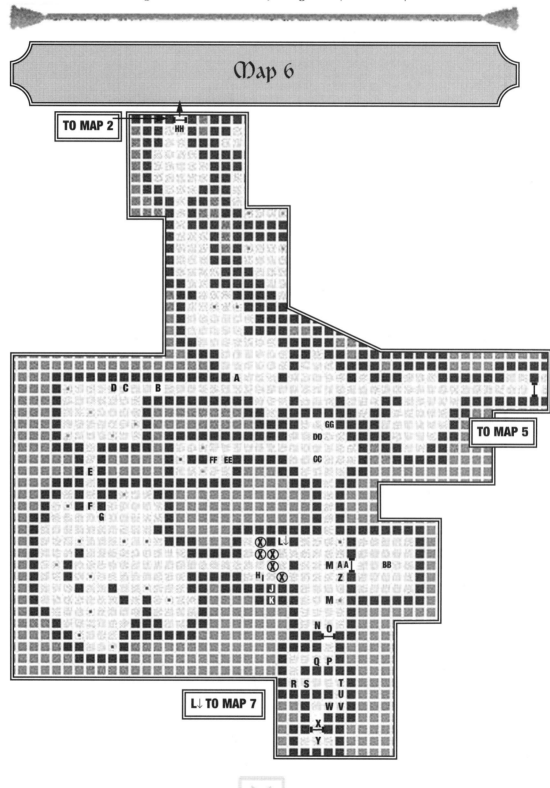

TO MAP 2

TO MAP 5

L↓ TO MAP 7

Map 7

A↑ TO MAP 6

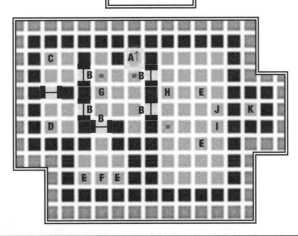

QUEST 5 (CONT.)

In the fire fountains outside the magick shop are two gold coins and yet another fire bomb, so get these and enter the shop. At last you can sell the fire bombs, spirit cap, and other less useful items for a large amount of cash. With this cash, buy the Kalan Gauntlet and Fury here because these items earn quite a profit if you sell them back at the axe-man weapon shop. Also, buy an emerald orb (+30 mana) and a staff of NETA (+25 mana) to help eliminate mana shortages, as well as for their nice healing functions that require no charges from the staff and transfer the character's mana directly into health points in one step — no more fumbling for potions in battle. Consult the shop guides in the previous chapter to find the best deals on quality armor and weapons, and make runs to the various shops to outfit the party properly for a change. The wall at 6GG disappears when approached from the south, allowing passage back to other areas and completely eliminating the need to cross the cemetery and haunted forest.

Once the party is well equipped and healed, go back to the temple via the magick shop and cross the room toward the haunted forest. Wield the serpent staff and prepare DES EW spells, or spend time to practice before taking the stairs down. Here you face two or three wraiths, and it is better to kill them now while you can escape up the stairs to heal. If you should happen to fall in when crossing the moving pit room, you'll be damaged and trapped with wraiths hounding you. After you kill them, waiting for the gates is no problem, so check the map and collect all the items, especially the hidden chest.

Now to finish the temple. Stand at the southeast edge of the covered pit room, and cast OH IR ROS, or use the magickal box since you can't sell it. Activate the scout map to monitor the pits, have the fire key in hand on the view screen, and make a mad dash for 6N with the keyboard arrow keys to place the key in the lock. If you're lucky, you can sidestep, open the door, and enter before a pit reaches you, but don't be surprised if you don't make it. Hence, the reason for cleaning out the wights first: at least one fall is almost guaranteed. Heal up after each fall. Once inside the Fire door, make another mad dash down the hall, open the unlocked door, get inside, grab Fury from the niche behind the tapestry, and wield the sword to fry the encroaching mummies with its fireballs. Or, take the casual approach by releasing the mummies one at a time and baking them with spell fireballs. Either way, get all the items from the niche and prepare for yet another mad dash to open the Air door. By now the Accelerate spell might have worn off, so cast another. Use the same method you used with the Fire key to place the Air key in the lock. Once inside the Air door, you'll find only a bartering table that spins the last clan key away from you no matter how fast you move or from what direction you sneak up on it. Simply place any coin on the table, and a ghostly shopkeeper barters the key to you. Then leave to barter with the regular shops once more, and go slay some thorn demon for steaks in preparation for the assault on the keep.

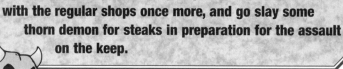

Quest 6

I can tell you are getting a bit bored with my narrative. Let me be kind and allow you to just look through my journal notes while I take the time to eat a bit and maybe have a spot of ale. I will tell you in a few moments about the bit that didn't make it into the journal: when we finally met Dragoth.

Quest 6

Objectives: Enter the castle, solve a gate puzzle, use the minion map, defeat the Vexirk, play with the cauldron, use the minion map again, remove the tech eyes, gather items, solve a door puzzle to reach the boiler room.

Maps: 8, 9, 10 and 11

Bring your best equipment and the four clan key pieces to the keep entrance and open the door. Save the game now and often because many of these puzzles offer no escape until they are solved. Once you are inside the door, it will close and lock behind you. Ahead of you is a skeleton on a floor trigger as a warning. Step forward on the trigger, then quickly step back to avoid the oncoming fireballs. This only happens once. The tech eye is decoration and watches passively, so being invisible won't help. Once the fireballs have passed, move into the alcove at 8I and turn north to face the gates. Two wall buttons are visible to the left and right. Press the left one first, then the right as quickly as possible. Then keep running forward and bounce off the gates until they open one after another. This method only gets you past two of the three gates, but no amount of experimenting will open all three at once, due to the time between pressing the switch and the actual opening of the gate. After reaching the third gate, face south. The gates will stay open as you approach them from the north. Stand beside the tech eye facing south, cast Accelerate, and make sure the mouse pointer is centered on the wall button directly ahead. Step forward and press the button, then run backward as fast as possible before the gates close. After clearing the third gate, get the gold key in the niche and walk — slowly — back through the gates to unlock the keep entrance door. Stepping into the button alcove again closes all the gates. To prevent having to deal with the gates again, move into the alcove one of the tall braziers, which won't trip the floor trigger and blocks entry.

Quest 6 (cont.)

Go back and collect the other items in the niche and behind the false wall. Go down the ladder nearby to grab the two fire bombs. Now you get to try out your new minion map. Climb back up the ladder, and step over to the square where the Tempest sword is lying in the center of a ring of pits. Activate the map, place an "X" on the spot where the sword is, and walk back out near the stairs. With the map still active, select the icon that depicts the minion moving away from the "X," and the minion will bring the sword to you. Otherwise, picking up Tempest opens a pit nearby which prevents normal escape with it.

Up the stairs in Map 9 await the Vexirk. Rest, practice, leave to barter, eat, or whatever is necessary to be at full strength before pulling the rope to call a Vexirk to open the gate. Once inside, do nothing to provoke them, including picking up items from the niches. Enter the smaller room to the west and stand patiently on the north side until the little rodents wander into the main room. When the smaller room is empty, start casting or activating as many Guard Minions as possible in the room, the more powerful the better. Assuming the room is still without Vexirk, go back to where you stood previously and get some sleep for mana and more minions, because when the fireworks start, the outer gate closes. Avoid the Vexirk with the staff at all costs because its burst of three fireballs can kill Champions quickly. Move around behind your minions to spread out their attacks, replace destroyed minions as necessary, and soon all the Vexirk will perish.

Now you get to play with the Vexirk cauldron. First, grab the Numen staff and put it in the Numen cauldron. Poof, it's recharged, making it the most valuable weapon by far, not to mention the +40 mana it provides. Next, get all the items from the surrounding niches, and place them in the pot as well. Poof, poof — you've made two more items: a serpent staff and the sword Blue Steele. Serpent staves, as the scroll directs, require a normal staff and a mana blossom. You can make as many of these as you have the supplies for. The Blue Steele used up the meteor metal sword blank, a red gem, a gold coin, and a spirit cap. Unfortunately, only one meteor metal is available.

Quest 6 (cont.)

With the Numen staff, both the gate and the door open up. Beyond the door is a pressure plate that very briefly opens the next door. Fortunately, this trigger responds to items dropped on it. Break out the minion map again, stand on the plate, and set an "X" here. Walk over to the closed door, drop any item like a coin that won't be missed, and select the map icon depicting a minion moving toward the "X". The minion then drops the item on the plate, allowing you to slip inside the door before it closes. Inside is a button on the door to open it permanently, assuming the item remains on the pressure plate.

The hall with the tech eyes is a deadly place indeed, because while the eyes are active, numerous huge fireballs wind their way down to incinerate everything in their path. So the simple solution is to disarm the tech eyes. Activate the scout map, and select the ROS enhancement to reveal false walls. The closest one at 10B also has a small, barely noticeable switch nearby that removes an otherwise solid wall section to allow access to yet another eye. Down the fireball hall is the second false wall, which leads to other small areas with more false walls and access to the other two tech eyes from behind, as well as to a niche containing a helm. Once the cover plates and eyes are removed, the fireball hall is safe to travel to the next section.

In this open area you'll find a fountain, a niche with a large gear and the Eye of Time, and even more false walls behind which are many niches with armor items and a teleport pad. Take this opportunity to port back to town and sell the items you don't need. If you have the extra cash, buy a vacuum fuse and four large gears from the axeman weapon shop — they will come in very handy soon. Port back, and walk up to the door near the niche. This is the first in a series of four doors that all require a large gear to open. Normally with the one gear provided in the niche you have to put in the gear, open the door, take the gear out, and move on to the next door before it closes and a pit opens beneath you. Bringing extra gears and keeping them "wielded" for quick movement saves time and leaves the doors unlocked in case you need to travel through again. The ladder down in this area is the way back up if you should happen to fall in a pit on the way. And if you lost the single gear doing so, another one appears in the niche to let you try again. Beyond the doors lies the beginning of the next quest, the boiler room.

Map 8

S↑ TO MAP 9

TO MAP 2

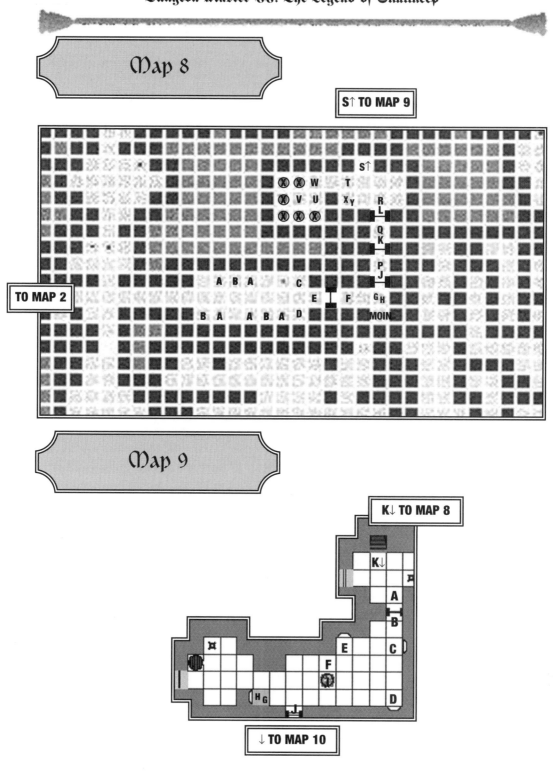

Map 9

K↓ TO MAP 8

↓ TO MAP 10

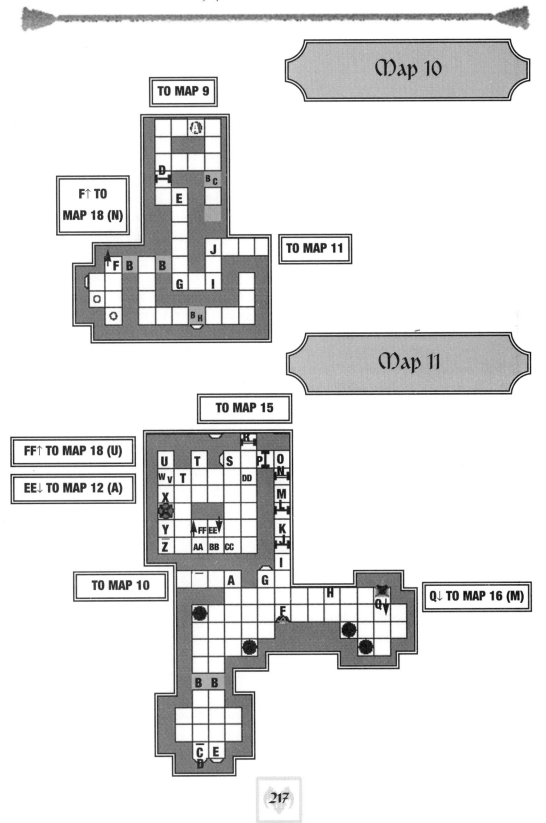

Map 10

TO MAP 9

F↑ TO MAP 18 (N)

TO MAP 11

Map 11

TO MAP 15

FF↑ TO MAP 18 (U)

EE↓ TO MAP 12 (A)

TO MAP 10

Q↓ TO MAP 16 (M)

Quest 7

QUEST 7

Objectives: Descend to the castle catacombs, defeat various nasties, retrieve the Earth key, save the rockies, get lots of gems and weapons, return to the boiler room.

SEE MAPS: 11, 12, 13 AND 14

Within the boiler room, an enemy attack minion and an enemy guard minion wait to annoy you with lightning bolts. Dispatch them, and close the blue minion portals with LO ZO. Get the Earth key from the niche and place it in the proper keyhole in the alcove, then press the button around the corner. This action unlocks the door at 11R but also opens a pit under the keyhole, into which the key is ejected and falls two levels down.

It would be unwise to follow due to the damage involved, so you'll have to take the "scenic" tour down because the same key opens a second door beyond the one you just unlocked. Grab the large gear and pull both levers in the room to the down position to lower the ladder and activate the boiler, but don't worry about the boiler not working because you'll have to fire it up from below. Heal up, port to town at the teleporter to set the port destination to here, and prepare to enter the catacombs.

Near the ladder down, an enemy guard minion stands watch over the furnace that fuels the boiler, so dispatch it. Consult the maps to find the exit back outside the keep on this level, and go there by pushing one or all of the huge boulders into the pits, sealing them. Terrorize the bats if you like. Once the way outside is opened, you can come and go through it as you please. Ignore the many pyros lying about; for now you have no use for them. Then use the ladder nearby and descend to Map 13, but remember this is a one-way trip down. Once on Map 13, consult the maps again. If you wish to fight numerous creatures for weapons and retrieve blue gems from the volcanic depths, head east and then north. Otherwise, heal up and prepare to face Dru Tan to the west and north.

There are two methods for killing Dru Tan, both of which are dangerous. But he must be killed because he carries the Blood key, which is the key to your freedom from the catacombs, as well as that of the rockies. He cannot be pushed or cajoled into the pits in the area, so you'll have to (a) kill him outright which is a dangerous and frustrating task, or (b) lure him into his own trap and escape it while he becomes trapped and dies.

The second choice is the easiest (and most entertaining) of the two, but it involves speed and knowledge of the trap. Study the map, and notice the hallway in the northwestern section of the Dru Tan area with two doors near each end. Evade Dru Tan, open and enter the door at 13R but don't bother to close it since Mr. Tan can rip through it. Just inside is a spiked wall that moves west when triggered by a pressure plate at 13T. Stand beside the plate without stepping on it. Turn to face the spiked wall, and as soon as Dru Tan enters the trap, quickly turn west and move all the way to the end, setting the trap in motion. Hopefully, Dru is caught in here as well, but at the end of the hall, a large button on the wall near the floor at 13U opens the door to the left, allowing you to escape. This button opens the door only once, so when you are outside the door, turn and close it behind you. If all goes well, Dru Tan gets forced down the hall and battered by the wall until he dies because the door will not open a second time from within. He can still cast poisons through the gate, so either get out of the line of fire or set a reflection field outside the door and stand behind it to watch his gruesome death. Once he dies, open the second door from the outside, go back to the first door and pull the lever beside it to reset the trap. The wall will move back to its original position, allowing you to safely pick up the Blood key within by entering the now open second door. Do not make the mistake of entering the trap without opening both doors or you will share Dru Tan's fate. If Dru manages to get out of the trap before it is set in motion, then you'll have to kill him the old fashioned way.

Now walk around the area and collect all the green gems, the emerald orb in the niche, and the Earth key before freeing the rockies. You may also go back to the east on this level and fight monsters for weapons and gems as previously mentioned, but this is not vital to the quest. Unlock the Blood door at 13O and let the rockies wander out. As soon as the way is reasonably clear, enter their prison and press the button inside, turning on a teleport field nearby. They will go toward it and enter, so you do the same. The teleporter sends you back up near the furnace at 12EE, where the rockies are trying to toss pyros into it. By now another enemy guard minion has blocked the furnace, so dispose of the minion by setting your own guard minions to either side, allowing the rockies to continue tossing fuel into the fire. Rockies aren't too bright and might toss pyros at you while at the same time greeting you with open hand gestures, so take pity on their tiny minds and let them do the work. Maneuver around them to climb the boiler room ladder once more, thus completing the catacomb quest.

Map 12

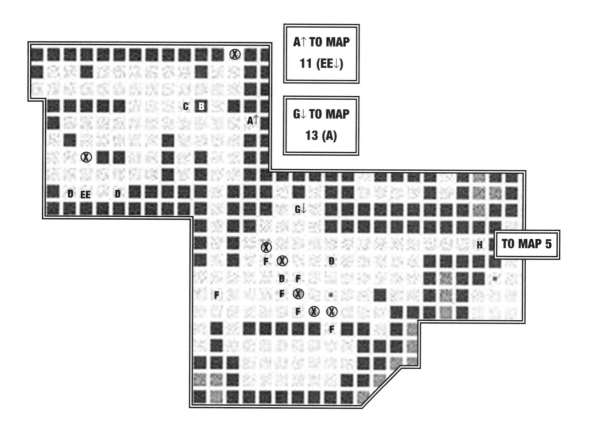

A↑ TO MAP
11 (EE↓)

G↓ TO MAP
13 (A)

TO MAP 5

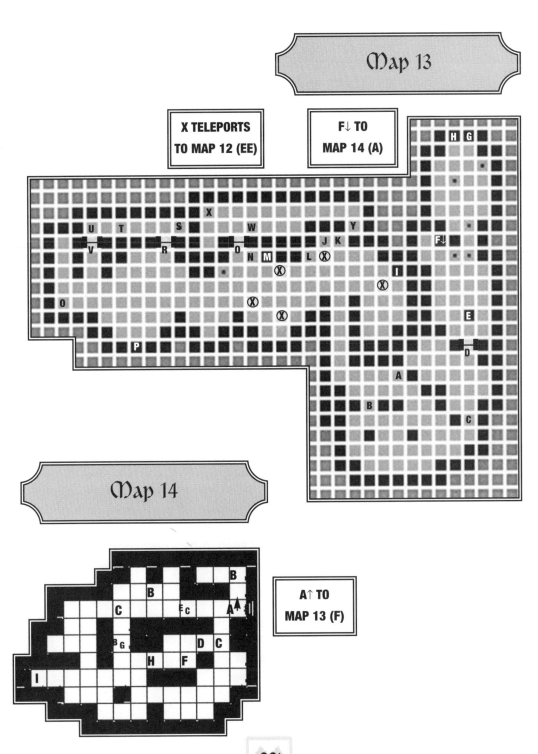

Map 13

X TELEPORTS
TO MAP 12 (EE)

F↓ TO
MAP 14 (A)

Map 14

A↑ TO
MAP 13 (F)

Quest 8

QUEST 8

Objectives: Optionally navigate the imp maze for armor, disarm the pit trap, deal with archer guards, get lots of slayer arrows, acquire the master key, solve a locked door maze to reach the pump room.

SEE MAPS: 15, 16, 17 AND 18 ON PAGES 224 AND 225

The boiler is still idle, so heed the advice of the signs and begin the climb up into the keep by unlocking the second Earth door at 11R. Close the blue portals with LO ZO again if you wish, but every time you change levels they return anyway. Inside, an enemy attack minion buzzes about, so dispatch it as usual.

Optional: The ladder down at 15D leads to the imp maze with tech armors lying around, but this also is not vital to completing the quest. If you wish, prepare a powerful fireball before going down, and as quickly as possible fire it down the long corridor that leads south to slay the imp before it has a chance to do any mischief. Grab the tech boots and press the button at 16B, closing off the hall and opening the way to another room. Enter and get the tech plate, then press the button facing south at 16D which activates a reflector and opens yet another passage out.

Press the other button to toggle the fireballs that the imp meant for you. Move through the reflector and follow this passage to a teleport field, which sends you back to the ladder from whence you came. A new passage west and south is now open, so follow it around to grab the last item in the maze, the tech poleyn at 16H. Then head back to the ladder. Note: If you didn't manage to kill the imp right away, then don't bother. This maze belongs to that imp, making it very difficult to get any of the items. Once back on Map 15, reaching the ladder up requires solving a pit trap puzzle. Near the niche containing a scout map at 15H is a ladder down and a pressure plate, beyond which lies an open pit. The plate activates ZO balls, which open and close the pit at great speed. The hard way to cross it is to cast quickness and try to time the closing so as to get across before it opens again. This method proves very time-, energy-, and health-consuming, as well as frustrating, but it is possible. The ladder provides a way back up should you fall in. The easy method is hinted at with the scout map provided: Activate the map, select the DAIN enhancement to see the source of the balls, activate a scout minion and stand on the plate. The ZO balls start flying and toggling the pit. Now send the scout minion across the pit to block the ZO balls by clicking on that spot on the map display. The trick is to block them with the pit closed, so if you fail on the first try, simply move the minion away and try again. Once the pit is closed safely, cross it and pull the lever to keep the pit closed for good. Heal and take the ladder up to Map 17.

This open area has dangerous archer guards, which lurk about and regenerate occasionally, and a strange floating chest. The guards will take the many slayer arrows from the two niches at 17J and 17S to fire at you, so run and grab them first.

The chest in the center of the room will produce a vacuum fuse if you kill it with fireballs, but it seems to know your intentions and evades skillfully, moving as far from you as possible as you chase it about. Hence, the purpose of buying a fuse from the axeman weapon shop to save you the trouble of running down the chest and killing it with fireballs.

The small, unlocked, room to the north, with pressure plates that release fireballs, was probably meant to bring down the chest, but this method ends up killing more party members than anything. Either way, there are two doors that require unlocking in this large area. The one to the far west, 17L, takes a vacuum fuse, which opens a small room containing a master key and items in niches behind false walls. Here you will also notice a raised ladder, which the master key won't unlock.

The other locked door at 17F requires both a large gear and the master key to open. A large gear is provided in a niche to the southwest, if you don't have any extras. Past this door is a corridor that leads to a lever puzzle, and past that a door requiring the master key again, so get it from the lock at 17E.

After going through the door, you will find yourself at Map 18 facing a fiendish looking puzzle. But what first appears as a complicated and frustrating trial-and-error puzzle is actually deceptively simple: The scout map on the floor here adds to the mystery, implying that it must be used when actually it isn't necessary. Go to each of the levers, toggle each at least a couple of times, and leave them all in the up position. This opens all the doors necessary to reach the pump room. On the way, abuse the large barrels with spells or weapons to break them open and retrieve the items within. The scout map does come in handy to navigate the twisting passages, but the minion need not be activated. The raised ladder at 18N, lowered with the nearby lever, leads down to the fireball hall area near the Numen. So if you need to recharge the Numen staff, do so now and return. After acquiring all the items from the barrels, open the pump room door at 18O with the master key. Inside there are several menial tasks to perform: Dispatch the waiting enemy minions if there are any, place a vacuum fuse in the appropriate slot at 18P, lower the ladder to the boiler room, activate the pumps by pulling the nearby levers and grab the Cross key from the niche.

Don't forget to retrieve the master key, for, as its name implies, it is used several times.

If necessary, go down the ladder to the boiler room and port back to town to barter and obtain supplies. Then take the keys back out to the room with the raised ladder at 17Q, and use the Cross key to lower it, completing this quest. Only two more to go.

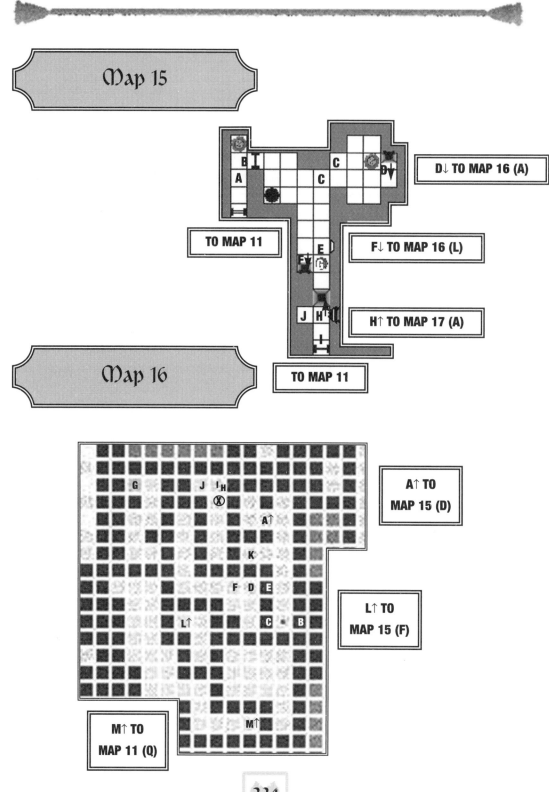

Map 15

D↓ TO MAP 16 (A)

TO MAP 11

F↓ TO MAP 16 (L)

H↑ TO MAP 17 (A)

Map 16

TO MAP 11

A↑ TO MAP 15 (D)

L↑ TO MAP 15 (F)

M↑ TO MAP 11 (Q)

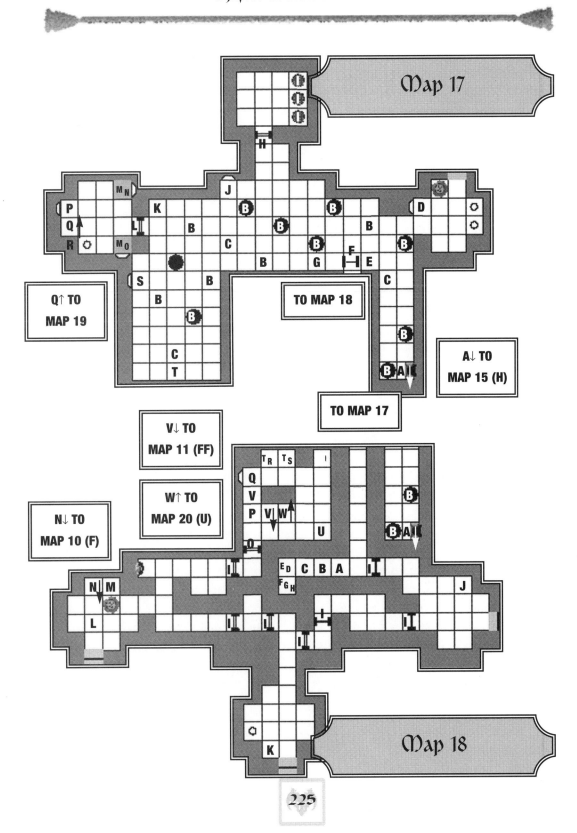

Map 17

Q↑ TO
MAP 19

TO MAP 18

A↓ TO
MAP 15 (H)

TO MAP 17

V↓ TO
MAP 11 (FF)

W↑ TO
MAP 20 (U)

N↓ TO
MAP 10 (F)

Map 18

Quest 9

QUEST 9

Objectives: Use the cross key to go up, blow up tables, negotiate a maze with rams that push you into pits, reach the valve room, solve the reflector puzzle, acquire lots of items for the last battle.

SEE MAPS: 19 AND 20 ON PAGES 228 AND 229

Up the ladder is a room full of regular tables. As usual, there is an easy way and a hard way to get past: You can skillfully maneuver them around like a sliding number puzzle, which takes much time and patience but is possible, or simply destroy them. Move one table in front of the ladder, stand back near the window, and splinter it with fireballs by detonating them on the wall directly behind it. Easier still is the hack-and-slash method with weapons.

Next is a truly frustrating puzzle with no easy solution: rams heads moving in and out of the walls, trying to push you into the many pits. There are several paths through the maze but all require the Accelerate spell and timing. Watch the rams carefully. You will notice that they tend to move slower when starting to move out, and again when returning to their starting position in the wall. The trick to getting past each of them is waiting until the in-stroke when it is almost back to the wall, then running past. If the ram is extended at any point, even starting to move back in, the ram forces you into a pit requiring you to go back up the Cross key ladder and start again. Timing is essential, and, as previously mentioned, there is no set path or easy method to get by. Surveying the maze with a scout minion helps somewhat, but it also gets pushed around a lot. By the time you reach the hallway leading to Map 20, the decision is yours whether to brave a couple more rams to reach tables with minions on them at 19L, M, and N, but "no" comes to mind. In the next room, which is on Map 20, are two mobile teleport fields. Depending on where you are when one hits you, you will be moved to nearby positions, usually where you don't really want to go. One of the fields places you facing a pit, so if you happened to be moving forward after the teleport, you fall in — requiring you to navigate the ram maze yet again. The honorable solution is to tread carefully by monitoring the fields with a map and avoiding them to get where you need to go.

The dishonorable (but more entertaining) solution is to again monitor them with a map, and run quickly from the entrance hall north into the reflector room where you can push the reflectors out and block the teleport fields. This will trap both of them into a corner since, they can't teleport or move into a space with a large obstacle. In order to accomplish this trap, you'll need all five reflectors, so it is time to solve the reflector puzzle.

Again, there is an honorable and a dishonorable method: the former entails moving and angling the reflectors about, by hand and with levers, so that when a fireball is fired northward with the pressure plate at 20M, it bounces all the way around the room and strikes its point of origin to remove the pits. This requires the center reflector to be moved while the fireball flies around.

As usual, the dishonorable method is much easier. Which it should be, or it wouldn't be the dishonorable method, now would it? Simply keep the scout map active, and play with the levers until the center and one of the side reflectors on the other side of the pits is angled to allow you to cast your own fireball north to strike the target with only two reflectors. Once the pits are gone, move the reflectors one at a time into the teleporter field room, restricting their movement until you can walk around the edge of the room without dealing with them at all.

Finishing the level now requires only menial tasks. The gate in the reflector room at 20Q appears locked, but in fact yields to a few fireballs, allowing entry and acquisition of quality armor. The door on the other side of the teleporter field room at 20G is indeed locked, and opening it requires the scout map. Activate a scout minion and move it to the space in the center of the four pits nearby. Get a copper coin and throw it at the minion. The coin will bounce off the minion and land neatly on the pressure plate beneath it, removing three of the pits and unlocking the door.

Inside is more armor and a Fury. Grab the bombs from the niches in the teleport room.

Lastly, open the valve room door at 20K with the master key, and this time you can leave it in the lock. Inside, get rid of any enemy minions, turn on the four valves, lower the ladder and go to the ladder up at 20P to the east and past the reflector room.

Only one quest now remains before your final encounter with Dragoth.

Map 19

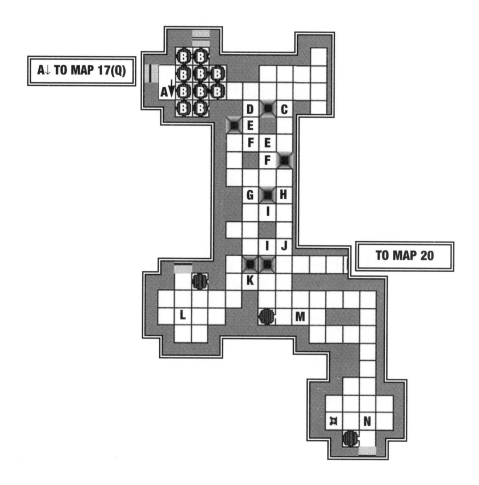

A↓ TO MAP 17(Q)

TO MAP 20

Map 20

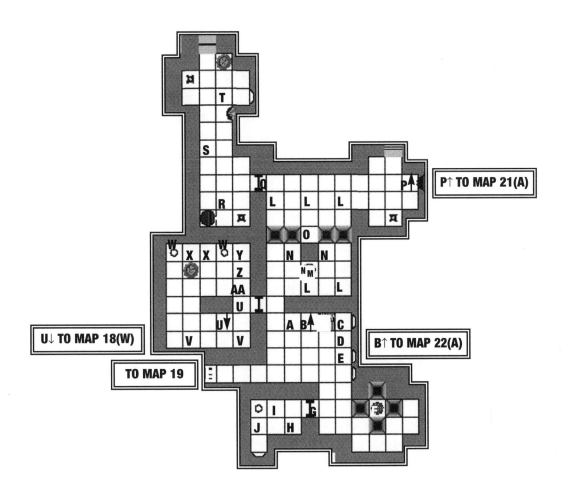

P↑ TO MAP 21(A)

U↓ TO MAP 18(W)

B↑ TO MAP 22(A)

TO MAP 19

Quest 10

QUEST 10

Objectives: Solve a key puzzle, get reflectors from a store room, position the reflectors, activate the devices (which may require a trip back to the catacombs), enter the dimensional portal.

SEE MAPS 21, 22 AND 23 ON PAGE 232 AND 233

Moving west on Map 21 beyond the ladder brings you to the "control" room, with various gauges depicting the activity, or lack thereof, of all the devices in the Keep. Don't be surprised if the boiler is inactive, because by now enemy guard minions have blocked the furnace in the catacombs again. The locked door at 21B requires the Onyx key to open it. To the north is the last teleport pad, allowing a trip to the outside for supplies. Further to the west is a hallway lined with lightning rods, with bursts of deadly lightning arcing between them. The situation looks more than a little grim.

Activate a map, cast accelerate, and watch the arcs for a pause that allows you to move through the hall. On the other side at 21K is a knife switch, which deactivates the lightning, and an odd circle on the floor. Beyond this circle is a niche containing two keys, both of which you need. However, only one of these keys is removable at a time. But, beware! The circle is a trap that, when activated, sucks everything into it, capturing the party in a most unpleasant way.

First, get the Onyx key at 21M. Get only the Onyx key: if you pick up the Skull key first, put it back and click the pointer directly on the other one. Take this key to the locked door at 21B and open it. The door stays open only while the key is in the lock, so leave it in and enter.

Moving on to Map 22, you will find that the area only has one inhabitant, an enemy attack minion, that you must kill. Now, you have two choices to activate the crystal device. Bet you can't guess what they are. Well, surprisingly, they are the honorable way, and the dishonorable way.

The honorable way requires a lot of walking and is the only 100 percent reliable solution, so it shall be covered first. Before entering the crystal chamber, lower the nearby ladder at 22A with the lever beside it, but don't climb down. Go back to the control room and get the Onyx key from the lock. Take the key back to the niche, being very careful to replace it before getting the Skull key. Take the Skull key back down the ladder to the reflector room, go out into the teleport field room, and climb the recently lowered ladder. Now enter the chamber, move past the central crystal and over to the locked gate at 22L.

Beside the gate is a keyhole for the Skull key. Unlocking it will activate a nearby teleport field. Enter the field and you find yourself inside the storage room, seemingly trapped. Fortunately the reflectors in the room are angled to allow the destruction of a table by fireballs launched eastward. Once the table is splintered, move the tall brazier into the space provided and hack the other table to bits. Now, open the gate from the inside and move the reflectors one at a time out into the crystal chamber.

On the floor are two round grates which mark the proper position of the two reflectors. Now all that remains is to activate the various devices in the room. These devices feed huge amounts of power through the crystal, opening a dimensional portal. First, enter the short hallway to the south of the crystal and pull the knife switch, then grab the attack minion on the floor. Next, walk out and pull the other knife switches, being careful to stand against the wall because pulling the switches releases a constant stream of deadly fireballs northward, where the reflectors angle them directly into the crystal. It is safe to walk around the edge of the room to the last device on the north side of the room, where the switch is inside an alcove. The lightning rod aimed at the crystal is powered by the boiler far below, so if the lightning rod doesn't work you'll have to trudge all the way down to the catacombs, take out the enemy guard minion blocking the furnace, and throw pyros into the furnace yourself because the rockies appear to be mulling about, dumbfounded. Trudge all the way back up and throw the final switch, sending lightning bolts and fireballs at once at the crystal, which finally opens the dimensional portal where Dragoth awaits.

Now for the dishonorable method: Forget fooling with the skull key or boilers and such, simply open the outer door with the Onyx key, walk straight in, throw all four switches in the room, whether they work or not, step inside the short hall south of the crystal, and turn north to face the crystal. Wield the almighty Numen staff and fire a burst of three small fireballs at it, then quickly turn around to watch with childish pride as the portal opens for you. Apparently the condition for opening the portal is having all the knife switches pulled down and three separate spell attacks strike the crystal at once, because you can go to the trouble of setting up the reflectors and fireballs, then simply hit the crystal with a cast lightning bolt rather than fooling with the boiler. The tight burst of three fireballs from the Numen staff is enough to satisfy this condition.

Optional: The ladder up in the crystal chamber leads to the rooftop, where several archer guards are breathlessly anticipating your arrival. Avoid satisfying their base urges by not going up there at all, or slay them for sport and close the blue minion portal opposite the ladder to prevent more from entering.

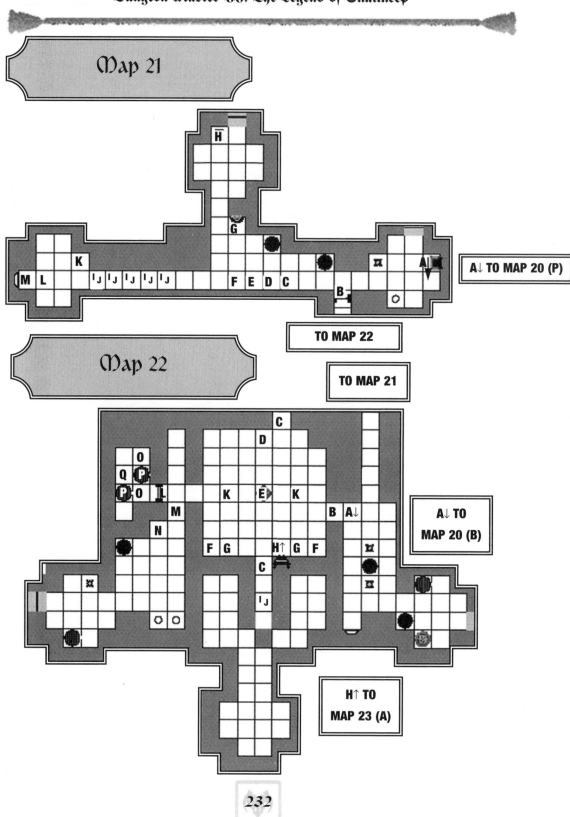

Map 21

Map 22

TO MAP 22

TO MAP 21

A↓ TO MAP 20 (P)

A↓ TO
MAP 20 (B)

H↑ TO
MAP 23 (A)

Map 23

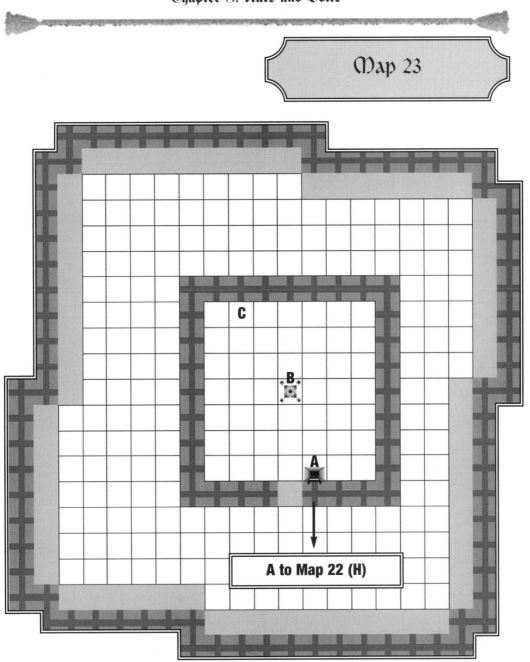

A to Map 22 (H)

Well, now, I bet you are waiting with bated breath to find out about how we fought Dragoth. Well, I will tell you all about it. Er, would you mind paying the Barkeep for that thorn demon steak? I think I dropped my change purse in the privy.

Death to Dragoth

I fired a burst of fireballs from the Numen staff, and the portal shimmered into existence in front of us.

"I like it!" I said, spinning my new staff in a short overhead arc.

"Oh, spirits, nothing worse than a wizard with an item-induced ego problem," mumbled Ravenblood.

I spun on him.

"I heard that!"

"Point that thing somewhere else," he said, shoving the end of my fine new staff aside. "I am going to have to remain unscorched if we are going to pull this off."

I reluctantly stood the staff upright.

"Now," he asked Tanic. "What's the plan!"

Tanic appraised the dimesional rift.

"I guess we go through to Dragoth's domain and fight him to the death. His or ours."

Ravenblood stared at the portal for a long moment.

"Well, guess you won't be needing me, then. So I'll just be toddling off..." he turned and ran directly into Zilch's massive chest. He turned back rapidly and took a couple of firm steps toward the portal.

"Through the portal it is, then," he finished.

We stepped through the portal.

The world of Dragoth was a forbidding place. Smells of rot and corruption filled the dank air, and the darkness crept in around the edges of the night, heavy enough to almost scrape our skin. Condensation immediately formed on our boots and equipment, beading and running downward in black rivulets.

"Well, it might not be a bad place to live, but I wouldn't want to vacation here," muttered Ravenblood.

"That is the bad part of this adventuring buisness — all the travel," I replied.

We were standing on a blue cloud pathway. Ravenblood took out the scout map, looked in all directions, and finally flipped a sliver piece.

"The signs say go south," he reported to Tanic.

"Signs! What kind of sign is that! You flipped a bloody coin."

"And it came up tails. A clear injunction from the gods to go south."

And so we marched south, finally coming to a moving walkway leading to a parapet.

I looked at the walkway.

"Okay, we jump," said Tanic.

I looked at the rate the walkway was moving.

"No, you jump. That thing is moving way to fast for me," I said. Then I lowered my voice a bit. "I get motion sickness, you know."

Tanic looked at me with a nasty glint in his eye. I considered showing him the wrong end of my new staff but thought better of it. Instead, I cast accelerate on the whole unit. Then we rocketed forward onto the pathway.

That was when the minons attacked.

I blew one out of the sky with my new staff.

"I love this staff!" I bellowed, sighting in on another of our flying attackers. Ravenblood reached up and knocked the staff aside before I fired.

"Save it," he said. "We don't need to hassle with these things. Save your power for Dragoth."

I really wanted to have the joy of blasting another of the minions to dust but had to agree with him.

We rushed onto the parapet. Off in the distance we could see the hulking, demonic form of Dragoth stalking about, with another section of moving walkway leading to him.

"Ugly mug," said Tanic.

"Yea. But he probably has a great personality," I said.

We negotiated the second moving walkway, finally coming face to face with Dragoth. I immediately fired the Numen staff, but he dodged out of the way and hurled a fireball back at me.

"Run left!" shouted Tanic, and we all scuttled to the left, the corona of the fireball just singing the edge of Ravenblood's robes.

"Big fireball. This might be a bit difficult," I said.

"Attack Minions. Let's hit him with the Attack Minions."

Ravenblood and I both started releasing Attack Minions, which swept forward to attack the hulking demon.

Dragoth, bellowing with rage, swatted at the minions and started marching toward us.

"You know, a drink would go down well about now," I said to Ravenblood.

With my fine new staff apparently unable to hit the unholy creature, I was more than a little nervous.

Tanic and Zilch, who had grown into passable spell-casters over the course of our adventure, fired off their much more limited array of Attack Minions. The minions joined ours in harrassing Dragoth. Ravenblood and I watched the performance of the minions carefully for a moment, then gave each other high fives and started to whoop.

"What's all the noise about," Tanic hissed in annoyance over his shoulder.

"It's all over but the fattened lamb bleating, Tanic. Look at that fine healthy color on our minions. Look at the way the demon is bleeding. The power balance is good enough. All we have to do is — " we all ran right to avoid a lightning bolt " — keep avoiding his attacks for a few more minutes."

Tanic fell silent and looked upset.

"This just won't do at all," he said after a moment.

"What won't do?" asked Ravenblood.

"This isn't an honorable way to kill him. We need to get in there and mix it up a bit."

"Surely you can't be even slightly serious. A body could get hurt that way."

"I am serious. This is no fit end to an epic. What will the storytellers say? 'And at the end of their great quest after many hard adventures and brilliant battles, they summoned magickal minions to pick Dragoth apart while they ran off to a safe distance and did their nails'?"

"Bravo!" I shouted, taking one of the last swigs of ale in my waterskin.

"No, it just won't do. We must kill him with steel."

"You're mad. We don't even know if steel would have any effect on him," I took a step back and pointed the Numen staff at him. Ravenblood readied a rune sequence and lined it up with Tanic. "Don't make me subdue you."

Zilch cleared his throat to speak, and I shifted the staff in a tight pattern between the two of them. Over their shoulders I could see that Dragoth was still taking a pounding.

"Uh, pardon me," Zilch said. "But empirical reasoning would seem to indicate that the probability of at least the vorpal blade being able to inflict damage on Dragoth approaches unity. While I am making this assessment based on anecdotal evidence, the sheer mass of the data would seem to lend a strong weight to our being able to damage him."

He cleared his throat again.

My jaw dropped.

I looked at Ravenblood and he at me. But we were obviously licked from the third word on. It wasn't the argument so much as the fact that he had made it. Imagine if your dog managed to bark out the runic syllables for a complex magick spell and blew up your cat. You would be too amazed to do anything but numbly sweep up the ashes and take a long drink. That is much the way we felt.

So I lowered the staff, Ravenblood dropped his runes back in his bag, and we just nodded mutely. Tanic smiled a great grin and pulled out his blade, turning to face Dragoth.

"Charge!" he yelled, and we ran forward.

We sidestepped a fireball on the way in and closed to shooting range with him.

That was when it got ugly.

Dragoth laid down another fireball that exploded point blank on Zilch and Tanic. They swung on him.

There is an argument, in retrospect, that maybe the vorpal sword did a small amount of damage to the demon. But, if so, I could not tell.

Dragoth reared back and fired yet another fireball. This one, like the last, caught Tanic and Zilch full on. Screaming in anguish and smelling of burning flesh, they both fell to the ground, a heap of smoking cinders.

Ravenblood and I snatched up their remains and backpedaled as rapidly as we could.

Then, as the sad tale contines, Ravenblood was too busy backtracking to watch Dragoth. A great lightning bolt fried him a few dozen feet away from the great demon. I dived for him and collected his remains.

This left me carrying the bones of my three fallen comrades, trying to avoid the great rampaging demon. And while moments before it looked as if our victory were a sure thing, well, I will tell you that my life was flashing before my eyes.

At this point, I was fairly sure I was dead, so I did something that would seem insane to the casual observer. That would only be because it was insane. Bones and all, I jumped off the edge of the area we were in, headlong into the abyss.

I fell for what seemed like an eternity. My gut wrenched with a magickal transition, and I landed back on the floor of the crystal chamber, the one with the magickal portal to Dragoth's world.

I pulled the last of the healing potions out of my pack and quaffed it. Then I started back for the village. On the altar there, I would be able to resurrect the remains of my comades.

And that ends the tale of our ill-fated attempt to defeat the demon. Destroyed by overheroics.

Eh, what's that! Oh, well, you really don't want to hear about that. Boring.

Well, if you insist.

It is a bit embarrassing, actually.

I went back into town with the full intention, I swear, of immediately resurrecting the rest of the party and going back to finish Dragoth. But somehow, on the long and hot way there, I decided it might be a wise move to get something along the lines a quick nip of ale.

There was, however, a slight problem. You don't go into a bar carrying the remains of your three dead comrades. And I knew, knew, mind you, that if I resurrected them right away they would want to go back and exact their revenge immediately, without having the sense to stop for a pint or two and rest.

So I needed to do something with the bodies, just briefly. Being something of a traditionalist, I buried them on outskirts of town. Then I went in just to have a quick one.

Well, one thing led to another. I met a couple of old mates and made a couple of new ones, and when the pub closed we all moved to someone's house and . . . well, I am sure you know how these things can get out of hand.

So a week later I went to look for them and, well, I, uh, lost them.

That is to say, I couldn't find where they were buried.

I really had the best intentions and fully desired to go back and kill Dragoth, right up to that bit where I, er, lost the party that way.

Oh, well, the past is the past, and I am sure you will do better. I wish you the best of luck and hope my little tale will help you on your quest. Unfortunately, I need to duck out the back. That man coming in the door resembles my landlord and there has been a slight mistake in his accounting. Somehow he seems to have the impression that I owe him money . . .

After entering the dimensional portal, the party is walking on blue clouds or something to that effect, and stepping off into the void teleports you outside the portal or sometimes to a random location at ground level outside the keep. The latter destination makes for a long walk back up the keep so it's best to avoid doing so unless leaving the room is imperative.

Activate a scout map and travel south until you reach the moving walkway. Cast accelerate, watch the map, and move across with it. By now, some enemy attack minions are buzzing you. Just ignore them. Another moving walkway separates you from the main area where Dragoth is stomping around waiting for you. Once you get across, the battle begins.

Sadly, there are no spectacular strategies to defeat Dragoth. Simply drop Guard Minions and keep an eye on Dragoth to sidestep incoming spells. He has 1,500 hit points and only spell attacks do any real harm to him. If the minions are doing a slow job or if Dragoth decides to engage in close combat, fry him with point-blank MON fireballs or the Numen staff. He is excellent at avoidance so don't try the fireballs at a distance of more than one space. And don't bother to push him off the edge; it won't work.

If one or two party members die, leave them dead as long as you still have a couple spell-casters to lay minions. Once the party is out of mana, walk off the edge, and most likely you'll return to the crystal room. Set a Guard Minion to keep enemy minions inside and go to sleep. It is unknown if Dragoth can heal himself, but it is better to be safe than sorry. Go back in to finish him as soon as possible.

Index